ENTRE-PRENEUR-SHIP

10 INSPIRING JOURNEYS INTO BUSINESS FROM ACROSS THE GLOBE

SUPERFAST
AUTHOR
WWW.SUPERFASTAUTHOR.COM

Disclaimer

This book has been published with all reasonable efforts taken to make the material error-free after the consent of the author. This book is sold subject to the condition that it shall not, by way of trade or otherwise, be lent, resold, or otherwise circulated without the copyright owner's prior written consent in any form of binding or cover other than that in which it is published and without a similar condition including this condition being imposed on the subsequent purchaser and without limiting the rights under copyright reserved above, no part of this publication maybe reproduced, stored in or introduced into a retrieval system or transmitted in any form or by any other means without the permission of the copyright owner.

Registered Office- 604, Mayur Vatika, Dapodi Pune 411001

Website: https://www.superfastauthor.com

Email: superfastauthor@gmail.com

First Published by SUPERFASTAUTHOR 2021

Copyright © ALL THE AUTHORS 2021

Title: ENTRE-PRENEUR-SHIP

All Rights Reserved.

ISBN 978-81-949350-3-2

LIMITS OF LIABILITY/DISCLAIMER OF WARRANTY

The Author of this book is solely responsible and liable for its content including but not limited to the views, representations, descriptions, statements, information, opinions and references. The information presented in this book is solely compiled by the Author from sources believed to be accurate and the Publisher assumes no responsibility for any errors or omissions. The information is not intended to replace or substitute professional advice.

The Content of this book shall not constitute or be construed or deemed to reflect the opinion or expression of the Publisher. Publisher of this book does not endorse or approve any content of this book or guarantee the reliability, accuracy or completeness of the content published herein and do not make any representations or warranties of any kind, express or implied, including but not limited to the implied warranties of merchantability, fitness for a particular purpose. The Publisher shall not be held liable whatsoever for any errors, omissions, whether such errors or omissions result from negligence, accident, or any other cause or claims for loss or damages of any kind, including without limitation, indirect or consequential loss or damage arising out of use, inability to use, or about the reliability, accuracy or sufficiency of the information contained in this book. All disputes are subject to Pune (Maharashtra - India) jurisdiction only.

ENTRE-PRENEUR-SHIP

10 INSPIRING JOURNEYS INTO BUSINESS
FROM ACROSS THE GLOBE

Book Dedication to Elisabeth Misner

O ur friend and colleague passed away during the writing stage and collaboration on this book. Beth's words of encouragement echo in our ears as we seek to help others on their own entrepreneurial journey.

"All my life I have found creative ways to incorporate services to others. From being a chiropractic assistant, managing special projects for BNI, and leading the prayer ministry in my church, my one question has always been: How can I help you? I want to know what I can do that will make things better for those whom I support and encourage."

Quote by *Elisabeth Misner*

Forewords

From the Desk of Ivan Misner

According to the Bureau of Labor Statistics (BLS)... BLS data show that approximately 20% of new businesses fail in the first two years in business, 45% in the first five years, and 65% in the first 10 years. Only 25% of new businesses will survive their 15th year or more in business. These statistics data have not changed much over time, and have been fairly consistent since the 1990s. There are many statistics around the world that show similar findings. This is startling and could put many people off the idea. This would be a travesty as many entrepreneurs have a positive and transformational experience in the world of self-employment. In this book, 10 successful entrepreneurs from different industries and countries have shared their journey that led them to success. This book is for those who want to start a business, for those who have already started a business, and to be frank, for those who are interested in what advice these inspirational leaders would give to their younger selves. I know the authors personally and I can tell you that this is a story to share. If I started out now then I would read this book.

Ivan R. Misner, Ph.D.
Founder of BNI
New York Times Bestselling Author

From the Desk of Graham Weihmiller

Entrepreneurs come from many backgrounds, but they all have the same goal in common – to put their mark on the world. In the pages that follow, you will see that the authors – who are world-class entrepreneurs themselves, have collectively supported thousands of businesses over the last decade alone.

Few authors in the world today have their unique vantage point. And they have identified important patterns to the success, they have created for themselves, and that they have enabled in others. I am thrilled that they are writing this book, and entrepreneurs all over the world will be better off for it.

One of my early mentors has once remarked that he wanted to make a billion dollars and then give it all away to charity. Whatever your plans are, these authors can help you create both success and significance. I have learned so much from them and so will you.

Enjoy this meaningful tutorial. Even more importantly, put their teachings to work for your business right away. I know I will. Onward!

Graham Weihmiller
Chairman & CEO of BNI

Preface

Likeminded, good, willing and positive people come together eventually! One by one or maybe ten in just a moment! You just need to put them together in proper conditions to make that magic happen: that is what we all call friendship. We all found ourselves in these conditions within BNI (Business Network International), the world's largest business networking organization. Thank you, BNI! (All ten of us are BNI Executive Directors).

All ten of us are leaders in our communities influencing business owners to "Change the Way the World does Business," thank you, Dr Ivan Misner, for sharing your vision and giving us a common purpose. Through our involvement and commitment with BNI, we started building these relationships, first individually and then in groups. This occurred during BNI Regional, National and International yearly events. Some of us met in the United States, others in the United Kingdom, and some also in Mexico, Brazil, Germany, Italy, Poland, and even in Thailand. However, as fate would have it, we all collided through our individual country representation on the Executive Director Founder's Circle for BNI globally.

In 2018, thanks to a Founder's Circle meeting in Dublin, we all kicked off a bond that has continued to strengthen. A year later, this bond grew even stronger, as friends summoned other friends, and the group got larger during the 2019 Founder's Circle meeting in Munich. Of course, relationships got even stronger with the time spent together during BNI´s 2019 Global Convention in Warsaw, Poland.

Some of us have been involved with BNI for more than 20 years. Some of us have had representation on the Founder's Circle for more than 10 years. Others were brand new to the Founder's Circle. We all have shared experiences and connections that brought us together, hence this book. We have a common purpose; we all wanted to further develop our business leadership within our countries. All with the same common philosophy of Givers Gain®, regardless of gender, age, nationality, culture, language, or religion.

As March 2020 approached and realizing our summer plans, we were quickly changing. We all met online one Saturday morning. We knew we would not be seeing each other in person for the near future. But we could use the BNI online platform to stay together, both personally and professionally, seeing each other through our video cameras. We all needed the support; we all needed to remain strong in order to be strong for our teams and business communities. We found the experience so beneficial we kept going. It became a recurrent Saturday meeting from Mexico City at 6 am to Perth, Western Australia, some 15 hours later. With all other time zones in between.

As we began sharing our varied experiences, we quickly realized that we could do more for each other. We continually discussed our business experience and the power of this unique network.

We started planning joint team events to connect and build relationships within our teams. We wanted to share with them the power of relationships. We organized international leadership workshops to discuss common problems and share solutions and good practices. Regardless of geography, regardless of the time zone, to keep helping our members and their families to prosper even during uncertain turbulent times.

We had a discussion on one of the Saturday calls – "what we wish we had known when we started our businesses." This brainstorming discussion ultimately led us to share our stories contained within the cover of this book. The book is a compilation of our global experiences to inspire others to endeavor into ENTREPRENEURSHIP; this first book is about ENTRE-preneurship. We wanted to share these compelling stories with you, and we hope you find this content useful to inspire you forward. We hope you find comfort that you are not alone on the entrepreneurial journey and to empower yourself to propel forward. From all of the ten authors, we wish you a happy and enjoyable reading.

Index

CHAPTER

One

When I close my eyes and walk throughout my childhood, there are two moments that I clearly remember.

The first was on a Saturday, in the afternoon, around 1 pm , I must have been around eight or nine years old.

On that morning, I had gone with my Father to a beam & block cement factory, where he was a bookkeeper. When we returned home for our traditional Saturday family lunch, he said: "Lito (he called me that), you know, one day, I would love to be known as Lito's Father. I don't want you to be known as the son of Mr. Afonso Vaz Afonso for a long time."

This challenge, his words, always echoed in my head, and maybe that's why, despite challenging situations, I never let anything move me away from that first goal. The power of those words, the way my Father let them flow out from his heart to me, was magic. Even when I am writing about this now, I can feel him by my side and I can hear him saying those words to me. Yes, words sent from your heart are powerful. We will get back to this soon.

The second incident was when I asked my parents for a

Zx Spectrum Computer in 1983. I remember my Father's reply: "It's not possible, my son, I can't! But you can use my home office computer, whenever free". The problem was that my dad's computer (in addition to not having games) had a green phosphor monitor; it was just black and green, and did not have graphics mode, only text! I do not know if you understand this when you can watch a movie on your mobile phone that has more power alone than all the computers existing in Portugal had in 1983. At that time, I wanted a Zx Spectrum to play at home as I did at my friends' house. I could have chosen to revolt and get angry and behave in a silly manner as children do when they do not get what they want. Today I am aware that at that moment, I spread the seed for resilience. My Father was always very positive. He usually said that nothing is impossible, that if I really want to achieve something, I should fight, try, and never give up, because that… that is forever!

So, he gave me a box of floppy disks (5 ¼ inches) and two manuals: one from CPM, the operating system prior to MSDOS, and the other from Microsoft Basic, a programming language. Once more, a new challenge: the manuals were in English, and I still had not learned English.

At that moment, I realized that I had two challenges:

getting my dad to be known as Lito's Father and learning a programming language through a book written in English.

Actually, there were three challenges: I also had to learn English by myself! Once again, I could have given up, but we never do that – we never give up!

In four months, I learned how to program by copying the examples from the book and making the necessary changes to understand each instruction's logic and function. Hours and hours of trial and error, and again trial and error, to get one tiny success! Here it was my resilience giving results. It was converting into a habit.

One day, with so many attempts followed by errors and errors and more errors, I hit the computer keyboard, a Kaypro 2X, my Father's computer at the time. As a consequence, a green line appeared on the screen! WoW! A LINE! That's when I discovered that there was a way to make graphics on that computer. I spent hours and hours hitting the keyboard, trying to reproduce that line. I had to do it carefully not to damage the computer as I was trying to learn how to start graphic mode and control it.

For me, a new world had opened up. A more complex programming world that, without picturing, turned me into an experienced programmer in interesting subjects that companies were looking for and ready to pay.

First, I did small jobs to solve some computer problems in companies to which my Father introduced me as someone capable of solving it. Then, the companies themselves asked my Father about me, and after that, they began to refer me to other companies.

My passion for this new world grew every day in a small city in Portugal's interior in the 1980s, mainly because I realized that I could create infinite worlds and develop solutions to solve complex problems.

I started to face problems as challenges, like "games" that I played to win. I knew that I would always win because I had found out that the real victory is in the process and not in the end. Do not get me wrong, I love to win also, but the passion of playing got me excited.

This passion made the journey enjoyable, thrilling, and rewarding. I believe that passion is the main component of an entrepreneur. Passion takes away hunger, thirst, sleep, and even pain. Passion is what allows us not to give up, to tolerate the pain that comes from a defeat, with a smile, the smile that comes when we look at the next challenge, that smile that gives us pleasure and cleans up the temporary pain of defeat and that makes us grow and ends up being an ally.

I soon started to transform my skills into money; I worked a lot for the Health area, developing all kinds of works that could be done using a computer: from slides - yes, slides! - those that were revealed and then projected; resumes and, of course, software and databases that were my first passion.

There are special years in our lives. The year 1988 was one of those in my life. In that year, three situations had an important effect on my life.

The first arose from the awareness that I could teach others to use a computer and make money from it to buy a better computer. I started spending time finding ways to turn my skills into money; I knew that I needed to earn to continue to buy books and better computers to continue learning, which could become my future (as in the beginning, it just seemed like a dream).

I was only sixteen but that did not stop me, so I went to a place where computer courses were taught and said I wanted to teach. At the reception, the lady told me to go away, that I was too young, and it was impossible for me to teach there. And, once again, I did not give up (we never give up!). I asked her to speak to the person in charge and told him that I was good at computers and I wanted to teach people how to use a computer. He looked at me and said, with a roguish smile, *"next week, the person in charge of computer training will come to Castelo Branco to recruit trainers, you will do an exam, and if you manage to get 100%, I'll give you a chance"*.

I think he did it to discourage me, but when I hugged him and effusively thanked for the opportunity he was giving me, he realized he was in trouble. I took the test and managed to get 100% and started teaching at night, making money consistently. My training was successful, and students began demanding for Antonio Afonso's trainings.

That was because they realized that all my training came directly from my heart, as I had learned in my earlier days from my Father. I only teach what I know, what I am in love with, so the words, sounds, and gestures are full of passion. The massive, spicy, tasty, universal, and amazing ingredient is the one everybody feels, and that is the reason why, if you don't love what you do, you need to keep looking for it and never stop till you find it.

The second remarkable event was in October of that same year, I presented one of my software for the first time at a medical congress, in Tróia - Portugal, to hundreds of doctors and health professionals. It was a system to help doctors to follow a UK protocol designed to treat gastric gastrointestinal bleeding. I took 6 months to develop it, using the computer they had in the Gastroenterology Service at Castelo Branco Hospital, who was my customer. I started every day after dinner and worked till almost

4 am in the morning; after that, I went to school at 8:40 am as it was also important for me to keep learning. During that time, I developed strong relations with the team of doctors and all the other staff from that Hospital Service. We spent many hours together because every time I had doubts, they had to explain them to me. This would become a significant achievement for them, for me, and especially for those who were suffering from that health problem.

I remember that my parents had offered me my first blazer and my first tie to wear at that event. But I forgot my blazer at home. What was amazing is that every doctor from the Gastroenterology Service of the city's Hospital whom I had been working with, realized that I was without a blazer. They also attended the event without a blazer so that I would not feel bad. I felt the taste of recognition and gratitude. Although I was only sixteen, they had made me a part of their team. At that moment I realized that it is not your title, it is not your age, it is not how many people you know, that makes the difference, it is how strong you are able to relate. It is not how much you know or who you are! It is how much you care and give to others.

The third event was a day when I got home to have lunch, coming from school, when my Mother told me that my Father was very happy and that I should ask him why he was that happy. When I sat down at the table, I asked him why he was so happy, and he answered in an emotional voice, saying; "you know, today, I went to the hospital to do an exam and, when I got to the reception, the lady looked at me and my ID, and asked me if I was Lito's Father and as if that was not enough when I answered yes, she called the doctors, introduced me to each one of them as Lito's Father and I was treated in an indescribable way. My son, now I'm Lito's Father. I feel so proud that you have made my dream come true." I remember the pride and happiness on my sister and parents' faces. I am the youngest child of four children and the only boy.

I did it!

I managed to accomplish my Father's desire, and I remember the taste of that moment, at that precise moment, 32 years ago.

Next summer, 1989, I went on vacation with a friend to Ericeira - Portugal. When we arrived and called home, his Mother told him that he had to go back, since his grandfather had died. I decided to stay there; I needed a break.

I had a lot of fun, but it also gave me plenty of time to think about my life.

I stayed at a campsite and Ericeira's best seafood restaurant was in front of it. Every day I rented a jet ski, ate on the beach, and most of the time I had dinner at that restaurant. I ate what I wanted, fresh fish, shrimps, seafood sausages, lobster. The price did not matter as I was charging 5€ per hour back to 1989. That is what people get today, even 31 years later. I was financially independent since I was 14.

One night, before dinner, I went to the cliff on the left side of the restaurant; I was watching the incredible sunset, the sun touching the sea, and listening to music on my Sony Walkman, thinking I was on top of the world and started to think: "What can I do more? Where to go?" I was so young and had come this far; I was making a lot of money, my family was proud of me, what else could I do? I looked at that sunset and the immensity of that ocean, and strange things crossed my mind. It was then that once again, my Father's words echoed in my head: "The difficulty is not reaching the top, anyone can do it, and the hard part is remaining there." At that moment, looking at the infinite ocean, I realized that I was significant only in my small town! Such a big world, so many challenges, so many battles to get in. So many failures to learn from and so many victories to celebrate! That was not going to be the last chapter of my life; I decided to live my life with passion and drive.

If you ever feel like I did in front of any big ocean, remember this, remember that you are the one who will write the next chapter of your life and that you can choose how it will look like.

What happens to us is not as important as how we choose to look at it, and the reaction that will generate. There is always an angle from which we can look at what is happening and find an opportunity.

An opportunity is a challenge; it is a game that you play with the tools you have and those you find necessary. Sometimes your tools are enough, sometimes not, and it will be necessary to get them. Be aware that the more you know, the more opportunities you will have to get new tools and skills that you will need next. Learning never stops, so we must be pro-active and learn every day. As Steve Jobs said, "we can't connect the dots looking forward; we can only connect them looking backward." That is why we need to stimulate our curiosity in different fields, the world is a complex system, and you never know when two different subjects intercept each other.

One year ago, my friend Mac Srinivasan shared with me that every successful entrepreneur goes through 3 phases, Survival, Stability, and Abundance, he captivated my attention, and I have been sharing a mix between what he shared and my vision about it.

The Survival phase is the one in which the money ends, and the end of the month is still to come. The Stability phase is the one in which the income already covers the costs, and the Abundance phase is one where you are truly successful. You share your success with those who never found their opportunities or were born in a place where opportunities are not for everyone or they need to be lucky to survive. The most critical phase is Stability. With stability, comfort rises and comfort is the biggest enemy of an entrepreneur. He starts to think that "I now deserve..." and it sometimes represents a step back to the Survival phase, and competitors love it! Those who use that comfort, that free time to analyse their product or service, to analyse market perspectives, probably will surprise their competitors, sometimes even the market, as innovation will lead them to the next phase, the Abundance one.

I hope that my stories not only inspire you but also remain as advice that you will remember when experiencing some similar situations.

Never forget that the way you look at things changes the things you look at, meaning that you choose your destiny. A great future is waiting for you; everything you need is already within. Unleash the power that is already inside of you, dare to dream, and have the courage to follow your passion.

Surround yourself with people that stand for the same core values, and you will live a life full of happiness because happiness is the path, not the destination. Never give up! I never do.

About António Afonso

António Afonso was born in Benguela –Angola in February 4th, 1972, he is an entrepreneur, CVO at Netsigma, a web design and software development company, Co-CEO at DeepEye, a Business Intelligence systems development company, they developed Reporting2You, a BI & Reporting application used by more than 300 BNI® franchisees all over the world to support their Directors Team and Leadership Teams, he is also CVO at UAB Interax, a Lituanian Startup with the impressive purpose of stopping unemployment in the world.

He has also worked as a trainer for several organizations since 1988. He has developed software from the age of 12 in different areas and presented his first software for the health industry at the age of 16.

In October 2010, he was invited by Orlando Caixeirinho to become a founding member of BNI® Confiança in which became its first Vice-President. In September 2011 he became the Executive Director of BNI® Pinhal & Alto Tejo.

António Afonso was the founder and first president of the Computer Science Center of the Polytechnic Institute of Guarda and member of the Advisory Council of that Institute. He is now a member of the governing bodies of AEBB – Associação Empresarial da Região Beira Baixa (Business Hub/ Business Association).

His biggest passion is his family, his wife Isabel, two daughters, Carlota, 16 years old and Maria Inês, 9 years old, and João Francisco, his son, 6 years old. He also loves travelling, cooking, reading, networking, and programming.

He loves being part of the amazing team of BNI Centro - Portugal and BNI South Brazil, which is changing the way the world does business.

CHAPTER

Two

Here is a shortcut to success? – It's the word "NO"

"Success is tumbling from failure to failure with no loss of enthusiasm."

– Winston Churchill

I like to introduce myself as a serial entrepreneur. I am not sure if that means I have failed at more businesses or that I have tried out my hand at more kinds of businesses. Sometimes I joke about it that being a serial entrepreneur is like being a serial killer? I have killed more businesses and moved on, and then I think it was necessary. So, now if you are wondering what all I have tried my hand at? I have at one time marketed floppy diskettes, plastic granules, pharmaceutical consumables and finally moved on to financial product distribution. Each one of this business was something which was started off by me right from the beginning and having no clients to start with.

However, going through business after business and building each one of them from almost a scratch and to make it grow enough to be able to sustain itself and take care of my family and me taught me one important thing, and this chapter is all about that.

So, if you are thinking of starting a new business or a new line in your business, this chapter is for you. In case if you already have a business, then it might be something which will remind you of how you must have also grown in the first place, and I hope it gives you the wind under your sails to take it to the next level.

If you are a manufacturer or even a service provider, at a start-up or a settled stage, the final success of any business lies in "SALES." Any business is finally about being able to generate revenue out of the product/service that you are offering to them.

Some of you might be thinking that is Sales important or Profits?

That is a matter of strategy of whether you want to create profits out of increasing sales volumes or through sales margin. In either of the strategy that you will choose, you need to be still able to approach the right prospects and market your product or services to them. Even if you wanted to increase the valuation of your company, you would need to show client acquisition.

"Sales are the inevitable reality that every entrepreneur has to face. It is the barometer of the success or failure of your business."

Every entrepreneur will also need other people to get his product or service out, but we are not going to focus on that here as this chapter is about sales persistence.

There are 2 lessons revolving around the word "NO" that I have learned through my sales journey, and they are as follows:

- Set your expectations of the number of "NO" you are ready to listen to.

- The answer is always "NO" till you ask.

  And I am going to discuss about these 2 thoughts in this chapter.

SET YOUR EXPECTATIONS OF THE NUMBER OF "NO" YOU ARE READY TO LISTEN TO

It was the year 2001, and I had taken an IRDA license to be an insurance salesperson and had tied up with the ICICI Prudential Life Insurance Company Ltd., which had recently started operations in my city (Pune) just about 2 months back. I was in the second batch of insurance advisors they had recruited.

In those times, the private life insurance company was a new industry, and they wanted to expand rapidly and capture the market share by having the "first movers" advantage. Hence, they trained us with some of the best possible means.

If you happened to be one of the performing and interested sales team members, we were also invited to special trainings from some really great national and international trainers on motivation. We were also trained in the sales and sales planning process. The model was simple, if you sold any policies, you got a commission or brokerage, or there was no compensation.

The best part was that as you sold more and got more clients, you were able to get compensation and various incentives, which were much more than even the basic sales compensation.

So, if you have got the idea, it was all about numbers acquisition and increasing sales.

I remember one such session held by a person from Malaysia. He was one of the best insurance salespeople in the world. He was also the best sales trainer in this industry, who was invited all over the world to speak to insurance salespeople to help them become successful in the industry. He owned a whole office building of 20 floors, which he had rented out to a multinational corporation. He lived in a million dollar penthouse, which was proof of his success. He had a team of 50 people and almost 15 employees. The final kicker was that, where possible, he used to travel between countries by helicopter to meet clients and his teams. He said that he used to hire a helicopter to save time. This all seemed like a dream.

When he was sharing his formula of how he had achieved this success and how he had achieved all this in just 10 years, he simply said that it was all about being "persistence."

He said that even now, his teams and employees had to start off by doing what he had done.

Every single day in the morning, he started off his day by making as many cold calls as were needed until he got one appointment. His only aim was to get one sales appointment every single day, and if he were going to take a day off, he would cover it the day before. He simply wanted to meet 365 new people every year.

He shared a formula with us on that day.

Normally it took 10 calls to get 1 or 2 appointments out of which it resulted in meeting 1 person. Meeting 5 to 6 such persons resulted in getting 1 sale.

This, he said, would guarantee 1 sale per week even if you started off from 0.

He told us that we would try this exercise, and each one of us had to call a minimum of 10 people and keep a record of the calls even if it were a "No." In fact, he said that he would strongly recommend that we picked up the phone directory or the yellow pages and started making the calls right then. He said that he was giving us the next

2 hours free to make the calls.

The aim was to get one appointment for the day after tomorrow as training ended the next day. (I will not go into the part where he taught us of how we should develop a script for the calls to make it easier for us and try out such different scripts, as this is not the main purpose of the learning I am talking about right now).

It seemed like a simple enough formula, and it does not seem difficult to just pick up the phone and make a call with a script.

I was wondering why would it take 2 hours?

Now, please remember that this was 2001 and so the number of spam or marketing calls being received on the phones was not like right now, and phone calls were still precious.

So, I picked up the yellow pages and started making the phone calls. I did not get the script fully right, but I was confident that I could deliver it.

I got the following results:

Call number 1 – "NO" without even letting me finish.

Call number 2 – "Not Interested" in between what I was

trying to say.

Call number 3 – Politely listened and said, "NO."

I was shocked and took a break. I went and had my lunch and then again got my courage up and started again.

Call number 4 – "No, where did you get my number from?" I said, "yellow pages," and the phone banged.

Call number 5 – Listened and said that he could not talk right now because of work but call back after 6 pm

Call number 6 – Asked me to call back after a week as he was traveling.

Call number 7 – "Please call me back tomorrow," as he did want to know more. So, no appointment.

Call number 8 – "Don't call me again. You are disturbing me."

By now, I was completely disappointed as it took me 5 mins between each call to make the next call.

I still had almost 15 mins left but did not have the heart to make even one more call for that day. In fact, I did not even feel like speaking to anyone on the phone for the whole day after all the no.

We went back into the training room, and the trainer looked at us and smiled and welcomed us back.

It was almost obvious that we were all strained and tensed, and there were lots of frowns on our faces in the room. For the first 15 to 20 mins, the trainer connected with each of us individually and asked us about ourselves and cracked a joke with each one of us or shared a personal, funny story. There was no mention of the calls.

He started the session with some jokes and funny stories and incidents about his life.

The mood lightened in the whole room, and you could see people smiling and start relaxing.

He then said that he would like to review the exercise and give the biggest prize, which was an imported bar of chocolate that he brought with him from Malaysia to one particular person who could not complete the exercise.

We were surprised. Failure being rewarded?

His first question was – "How many of you were not able to make all the 10 calls?".

Out of the 25 people in the room, about 8 got up. This included me also as I had stopped at 8 calls.

His second question was – "From the other 17 people, how many of you got an appointment?"

10 people said, "Yes."

His third question was – "Whom did you call?"

Out of the 10, at least 7 replied that they called people they already knew, as he had asked to make a min of 10 calls and get a YES.

His fourth question was – He asked the rest of the 7 who had made all the 10 calls, "Whom did you call?"

They replied, people they knew. They spoke to them about insurance but could not ask for an appointment; however, the other person said, "let's meet to catch up," and they counted that as a YES.

His last question was – For the 8 who did not complete the calls, "tell me about how many calls you made and what the replies were?"

Each one of us answered.

All of the 8 who had been unable to complete the 10 calls had decided to follow what the trainer had recommended to us and made calls to strangers from the phone directory or yellow pages.

Out of the 8 people, I had made the maximum number of calls before giving up. I had got the maximum number of "NO" compared to the others, and only 2 had said "call me back" out of the 8 calls that I had made.

I felt like a loser again.

That is when the trainer asked everyone to give me round of applause and called me to come to the front of the room and handed me the chocolate. He said that I had won as I had shown the power to absorb the greatest number of "NO."

This was one of the greatest learnings of my life.

"To get a YES, one must be ready to go through a greater number of "NO."

My motto since that day has become –

"Every time we try to reach out to someone, and we hear a NO, we get a step closer to our YES as it gets the NO out of the way."

The more I look back at my life, the more I remember that each time I started building a new business, this one mantra of life helped me open doors throughout my life.

Though I have shared an example of a business which was to do with direct consumer sales, the same actually has worked even better for me for institutional and business to business sales.

In the plastic granules business and the pharmaceutical business, I was dealing with other businesses and at times with large companies, and this worked for me even over there. I would pick up the phone and request to speak to the purchasing department and ask for an appointment to meet up to discuss about the products I was marketing. Sometimes, it took me almost 3 to 4 times of follow up to get an appointment with them and get in front of them.

I did get a lot of "NO" on the way but, I did not stop.

My simple suggestion to any business owner today would be that one should never forget our power of not getting discouraged by a NO.

If you have the conviction in your product or service and if you are sure that you are providing a solution, which can help the people who need it, then it's time to start finding your formula of success and understanding how many "NO" means that you will succeed.

Till the time you collect the statistics of what is the formula for your business, you can go with the one which worked for most of us, which is 10:1. One yes out of 10 people you meet, and with time this score will surely drop.

So, maintain a simple ledger where you write down every call you make for sales on a daily basis.

Keep a separate page for each and every day.

You could make columns like this to help you keep a track.

DATE OF CALL	CALL NUMBER FOR THE DAY	NAME	NUMBER	YES OR NO	WHY NO	FOLLOW UP NEEDED

Let me also talk about the other side of the coin.

If currently your statistics for getting a yes is 1:1, which means that every call leads to success, all I can say is that then you are making far too few calls. Maybe, you might have to examine your sales cycle and if you have completed the cycle of going from where you started – afraid to hear a NO.

It might be time to step out on a new adventure or to reach out to a new set of clients or start a new vertical. As, when you listen to those NO, you will grow.

I would just like to add as a footnote to this section that when I say that you will get a YES going through your NO, it is really important to ensure that you do have a script. Also, if you can have multiple scripts ready based on whom you are speaking to, that will increase your hit ratio.

That, of course, is a topic for another book and I have also written a whole book on this topic, and you could read that, and I hope it can help you with that part of your sales process.

The book is called "It Starts with You." It is available on Amazon and also on Kindle.

THE ANSWER IS ALWAYS "NO" TILL YOU ASK

This chapter was more about how to get yourself ready for the "NO" if you want to become successful in business. There is a small sub-point that I thought I would cover with this as a side note. This might help you to get less of those "NO" with time, as the idea is not to make you think that entrepreneurship is tough, though it is, but there are ways to make it easy too.

I spoke about how I was making the calls when I was marketing plastic granules and pharmaceutical consumables. Most often than not, I was able to get an appointment with a lot of the companies without knowing them at all through a cold call.

I would go into the meeting ready to deliver my complete sales-pitch, but it was not giving me the results required. I did understand that it was my fear of NO, which was still on my mind. Now the fear of NO had shifted from getting an appointment to closing the sale.

So, there were two things I learned to shift with time, and they were building the relationships as taught by my friend Paulo Corsi in his chapter. This helped me build a relationship with the person without the fear of being rejected, and this helped to convert a lot of "could be" NO to "let us speak about it after a few days" or when their contract got over for this period.

This also gave me the courage to ask for the closing of the sale, "Because if you do not ask, the answer is always NO."

The last learning, I can share with you is something that works more for the industrial or business to business sales. Even when people say NO, it is still a good idea to ask them of whom or what they think they would suggest I should try and meet in the industry or what I should do to get more orders. Wherever I took the time to build the relationships, they would go out of the way to help me by giving me valuable suggestions about who could be a good client for me. Some of them went out of their way to let me use their names and made phone calls for me to help me get an appointment.

So, ask for the sales with a closing pitch and then surely do ask for referrals and recommendations.

A lot of you have started a business or are planning to start a business because you have had some inspiration but do remember if you want this to succeed, you will also need the persistence and perseverance.

The power to listen to many "NO" as they are the stepping stones to all the "YES" that will make you successful.

Let me end with the words of Steve Jobs -

"I'm convinced that about half of what separates the successful entrepreneurs from the non-successful ones is pure perseverance."

About Bharat Daga

Bharat Daga is the bestselling author of the book "It Starts with You", which is a book on a subject very close to his heart, which is to bring together communications and personal connections for finding success.

Bharat is the Executive Director in BNI of the Pune East region of India. Through BNI he helps business owners to succeed through referral marketing and grow their business through building relationships with their contacts and connects.

He has been a serial entrepreneur involved in marketing of various products and services like Textiles, Computer Peripherals, Import and Export of commodities, Pharma Consumables, Financial products.

His Professional Desire is to create a community of business owners who work as one big team to help each other succeed together and live a happy life.

Bharat believes that new experiences are one of the best forms of learning and is what keeps him alive and motivated. He says that this is why he has gone sky diving, hot air ballooning, scuba-diving, river rafting, jumping of buildings. He feels that his other experience of new is through food and he loves trying out weird foods and drink across the world through his passion of travelling with his wife Yamini.

CHAPTER

Three

It wasn't my original idea

I never planned to be an entrepreneur or a business owner.

When I think about it, I can remember many things I dreamed of becoming or achieving in life depending on my age - professional basketball player or extreme athlete, diplomat, chef, partner of a big law firm- but becoming an entrepreneur and business owner was not among my wishes. I would like to share with you some of the strongest life lessons I have learnt along the way, after years of hitting walls, falling in holes and hundreds of bad choices. Hopefully, you will agree with me that it is all about TRUST and ATTITUDE, it is always about you and the way you face your life and its circumstances! Life is built on our decisions and we are not perfect individuals. So, it is natural to make mistakes while making decisions. Nevertheless, we are truly capable of shaping our future and changing our faith, by transforming a wrong or bad decision into knowledge. It becomes easier when TRUST and ATTITUDE collide in the correct way and proportion.

The right combination of both factors multiplies results, by exponentially creating a positive spiral of growth, wealth, and wellness around life. You are the vortex and I want to share with you how I discovered it for myself, how life taught me to find it within me. Are you successful now?

I believe success is an attitude towards life, and not a goal of life. Think about it, if success were a goal, who would be the referee? Which are the parameters to achieve it?

Regarding a successful mind-set or attitude, here is my secret combination, the key to be able to activate the Growth Spiral: 1. Self-confidence, related to the way and amount of trust you have in yourself; and 2. Responsibility over my actions and their consequences, related to the attitude towards life, where you acknowledge you are The Cause and not The Effect, you are always responsible, always! It took me 24 years and a near to death experience to start understanding this.

I have not planned it, nor dreamed it, but today I´m CEO and the main shareholder of 3 companies, leader of a community of +700 business owners and partner in a global legal organization with +160 lawyers in 60 countries. What happened? It all started in my childhood, regardless of everything my parents sacrificed for me, for whom I am humbled and thankful now. My father became an entrepreneur and started his own business when I was around 5 years old and concentrated fully on growing it for the next 20 years. He has not been around much, working all the time to ensure a better life for us. He accomplished that, and much more. But at that time, as a child, I did not get quality time with him and our relationship paid the prize. I went to school before he had woken and went to sleep before he had come back home. To be fair, I must admit that I was not a good and disciplined student, as I never tried my hardest and had reports practically every day of the week. My relationship with my father became difficult and we drifted apart easily. As a consequence, I rejected everything that had to do with him: he wanted me to play tennis, I played basketball; he is an engineer, I decided to study law; he was an entrepreneur and business owner and I rejected that too.

I was wrong, my attitude had been wrong for years. When I undetstood this, things started to change for me. For years, I had chosen to focus on everything that my father was not, but I wanted him to be. I lived regretting, demanding, ambitioning, and growing sad and empty based on those things I did not get. Even worse, I was assigning all the guilt to my father. Sadly, with this kind of attitude I was not able to see all the love within the sacrifices of him working 12-15 hours daily. Life has taught me that even the closest relationships, parents for example, have the right to be imperfect and mistaken. What if they don't realize they are doing something wrong? Is that truly a mistake? Does it depend on the consequences or on the intentions? Every time we feel mistreated or hurt, we usually choose to be proud, put the guard up and search for the guilty. But that feeling is based on our attitude towards the situation, not necessarily related to the original intention. If we change our attitude, we can change the outcome! Try stepping back and be humble. By being humble you get to be opened to more information, open enough to be able to respect different ways to see, solve and understand life. Maybe, that mistreatment is just your perception. If we are thriving to move forward towards our happiness, accepting that happiness is our responsibility, does it really matter who is right or wrong? The key to owning the consequences lies in the way we choose to react upon each situation, this way you can take control and full responsibility. Because we can never be certain of someone else´s intentions, and happiness is particularly important to be someone else's responsibility. So, external factors can affect and interrupt your process towards happiness only if you give that responsibility away. The impulse or motivation of external factors affecting us will never be clear nor will they be our responsibility; do not lose time figuring out the intention. Instead, analize if there is something you could have done to provoke a different outcome. It's also critical to take guilt out of the equation. In our growth process we always need to add factors that allow us to develop, guilt is a negative and obscure factor, it is like an anchor to the past that makes it difficult to advance forward. Identifying who is guilty is only important in court, life is a much better judge, and it rules without a jury. It does not matter who is guilty but who is responsible for making the best out of each situation: YOU!

Other people's actions will become part of your luggage, choose them wisely because many of them will add impulse but some others will distract you and even change the course without you knowing. For example, on the other side of guilt's coin, it is recognition! This enlightening factor of development has helped me identify and absorb all the positive teachings of the negative experiences. We are never alone through our life's journey and it is especially important to identify, acknowledge, thank, and give credit to those who directly and indirectly have added something. But we are the sum of all that knowledge.

At present, I have a great relationship with my father, and I am glad that he is still around to be able to read this, because his actions have been my guide. My parents have been there for me as my main pillar, they have been my lighthouse and they have stood still for me regardless of my mistakes, always a safe place to come back to. Honor your parents, family, friends, teachers, and mentors, make them proud, and try hard to show them that their efforts paid off. Your accomplishments are the best way to show it. But stay humble. Don´t judge them too hard, just trust in love, their love! We need to trust in the existence of this kind of love, to be able to share it later with others, unselfish giving. Family love happens to be the main source to self-acceptance and self-love, which are then necessary to build your character and self-confidence. Accomplish it and you will cherish life and serve others, so make peace with your past in order to lose the anchors.

Trust life as a teacher, find yourself, love yourself, trust yourself; be brave, be bold, and seize life. Maybe you can start by taking a leap of faith and believe that you can! This book is all about that. Please remember that I did not want to be a business owner, I never planned it, but life knew better. Would you agree that in our present societies it is difficult to be yourself? Common life is already planned and structured, it is easy to guide your life and actions following someone else´s plan. We grow up in an environment, built to follow other people´s knowledge, experiences, and goals, and we walk through life trying to achieve and accomplish the perfect profile and grow to become what is expected of us. That is ok for some but not for entrepreneurs and leaders. In the first 24 years of my life, I fought hard to belong and be accepted. Fitting in, knowing my place, and accepting what was expected of me made me very unhappy and stressed. Regularly, I was being told that I was irresponsible or just not good enough. For a long time, I believed those external opinions! So, I tried hard to be better and fulfil those expectations. But as it turned out, many of the things I was pushed to change back then, today are strong parts of my character and identity. For example, primary school was painful for me; I was very bad in every part of it. It was tough for me to build relationships. I have always been very giving, many times worried about others more than myself, sensitive, romantic, honest, caring, imaginative to the point of being caught dreaming awake (distracted all the time, they said). A constant remark was that all those characteristics were more suitable for a girl than a boy and that I needed to behave more like a man if I wanted all the abuse to stop and if I wanted to be liked and "popular." Today, I can assure you that I do not have any problems with that, and no one dares to doubt my masculinity. Back then, I was not good with women either. I was continuously rejected when I wanted to develop a relationship to the "boyfriends" stage. I believe the explanation for this is obvious: I was too romantic and sensitive, not "aggressive" and "alpha" enough! So, girls appreciated me as a friend, but not appealing enough to go further. These days my passion comes from being romantic towards the concepts of love and humanity and being sensitive still motivates me to help others.

On the learning aspect of school, I was not successful

either. Imagine that I had a teacher who implemented a classroom official bulling technique, named "The Box for the Stupid Questions" and guess who was the champion of that? Right, it was Edgar, 8 out of 10 times! I have had that teacher for 3 years! So, years passed, and my grades did not improve; I grew distracted and absent most of the time. My notebooks and my school agenda were full of red notes to my parents because I never did my homework. I started hiding all this and lying to my parents and my teachers. I had put myself in a very negative spiral and did not know how to get out; I was so down that it was impossible to get better. My family also did not have a clue how to help me, and obviously, it affected the whole family dynamic and relationships. When I was little, my parents used to call me "smiles," and all the smiles were gone. In their desperation, my parents took me to the psychologist, and I was diagnosed with ADD (Attention Deficit Disorder), which was very new back then. The doctor recommended a 2-month treatment that required me to be completely unstressed; therefore, not going to school. My parents agreed, considering that my school year was going to the drain anyway. For me, this was scary because that meant accepting total failure, my current situation was bad and uncomfortable, but that was all I had and knew.

But life is wise. This gave me a chance to breathe.

I must confess that this was a turning point in my life because it took me out of the situation. I was too young and inexperienced to take myself out, but smart enough to learn and evolve to adapt and avoid repeating. I flunked the school year and had to repeat it, they might say I lost one year of my life, but I actually won life back. This was the first of many second chances that life has given to me. Be brave and trust yourself; it does not matter if you are still not confident enough, be courageous, and trust that you will find your light. Be aware that you have been living in a comfort zone, your path has been guided by other's lights, but those others are walking and constructing their own paths. You can always choose to build a path parallel to others and even make others' paths your own. But be true to yourself and do not expect much out of that.

If you seek to be the architect of your palace, the captain of your ship, then let us go further. We first have to be successful to get confident; yes, you have to build momentum, small wins, small successes, one after another. And some failures in between to stay humble and keep learning. So, with this second chance, I left the past behind and ignited the Growth Spiral. I was repeating 6th grade, but I felt bigger and stronger; this time, I believed in me, I knew and understood the game much better, and I had a plan. Always identify your strengths and weaknesses and evaluate how they play under the current situation. Before starting that year at school, I decided that I would never go through that kind of negative spiral again, and I have not. But that does not mean other kinds of bumps and bruises weren't around the corner. I shadowed the romantic and sensitive part of me; I drew less, dreamed less, and almost forgot how to imagine. I invested all that time socializing and focusing on sports. I started making a lot of friends and became "popular." I finally got to have a girlfriend, the most beautiful girl! There was no more bullying, and grades were ok. I went on to middle school, became captain of the basketball team, and won many track competitions.

At last, I was growing confident, but at what price? And under what structure? Never forget, building your path under shared light is risky. What will happen when you disagree with the light holder? Darkness again, perhaps?

Do you still remember the title of this chapter? Let us remember that becoming an entrepreneur or and business owner was not my idea. But then again, if we analyze closely, we will see that I had been living by someone else's ideas and was becoming successful in that. But did that make me happy? When I decided to adapt my character to fit in, I started walking a dangerous path. After finishing high school, it was time for University, and choosing a profession was not easy. I did not want to become an engineer; I wanted something fun and creative. Gastronomy was very appealing, but then others' opinions were that I would starve to death if I studied to be a Chef and that I should study something more promising. I liked the pursuit of justice, so I chose to study Law. I also liked languages and diplomacy, so I chose International Relationships. I was lucky because I was accepted in one of the best universities in Mexico City to study both careers at the same time and getting both degrees in only 5 years. I was so proud and happy that nothing else mattered. I come from a background of engineers; there were no lawyers before me in my family. I quickly realized that without a lawyer's background around me, I had a disadvantage, and I had to overcome it. So, I decided to focus only on Law and quitted International Relationships, I also started working as a paralegal.

Now I was in pursuit of the dream! Whose dream? What dream? The perfect dream, the one generally known and accepted: become a professional, grow successful, get a wife, and build a family. Right? I was on the right track again; it seemed. I started working hard to become a Corporate Lawyer and, someday, maybe a partner in a big law firm. Every day I went to school for my 7:00 am class, 25 km away from home, then went to work; back to school until 10:00 pm, went back home to do homework and study, slept for 3 to 5 hours, and started all over again. It was all worth it because I was investing and building my future, pursuing THE DREAM. Apparently, I was on the right track, I was in last semester about to finish Law School; I had the dream girlfriend, she was 4 years older than me, already successful working as a national manager for one of the biggest companies in Mexico; and I was working in one of the 5 best law firms in Mexico City. Then it happened. I had a brain stroke! Darkness again, real darkness this time. But why? Everything was falling into place so well. Never grow too proud to forget that you are still just human. There are many more important things than accumulating achievements.

The brain stroke put my life on hold for almost three years. But it gave me the chance to be reborn with a clean sheet. The neurologist diagnosed the cause to be stress! At the age of 24, he prohibited me from going back to work for someone else because I had to be able to manage my stress levels. The 4-year work, the pursuit of THE DREAM, it all came crumbling down and disappeared.

Good thing it was not MY DREAM!

It took me a while to recover; it took me even more to understand and accept what had happened. But now I get it, and I have the chance to share it with you.

Life is wise. I was diminishing myself; I was capable of more and needed to start building my path under my lights! I had to build my ship and get behind the steering. This near to death experience gave me the chance to question everything, to cancel everything that I did not agree with; to love and respect myself as an imperfect being. Again, I am sensitive, caring, giving, and I dream a lot! It made me powerful because I love myself, I trust myself, and I am responsible for my path and journey.

That is how I became an entrepreneur and business owner. It was not my original idea, but now it is mine, it's MY DREAM I'm building..

About Edgar Ramirez

Edgar is a unique person; he is a survivor. Edgar believes that knowledge can be shared but truth can only be found. Failure, doubt and misbelieve have been the most powerful teachers for him.

Edgar was born in a warm Mexican middle-class family. Second son of great giving parents Rodolfo and Ednna. From them he learned family love, sacrifice, loyalty, responsibility and hard work; he also learned that the best investment is quality education of his children, as he benefited from this his whole life considering that his parents always prioritized their sons' tuition.

Edgar is a citizen of the world; he feels comfortable among people of other cultures and nationalities. Due to his multicultural education he finds it easy to understand and relate to other ways of thinking and doing. Edgar speaks Spanish, English, and German.

Edgar studied law and worked in several important law firms until 2004 when he suffered a brain stroke at age 24, an important turning point in his life. After recovering, he went independent and in 2009 he started his own company.

In 2008 Edgar was invited to join BNI in Mexico City. After 6 months, the Givers Gain philosophy made sense to him. In 2010 he became Director Consultant for BNI Mexico. Today Edgar owns 3 BNI franchises and leads a community of over 700 business owners, CEO of 2 companies, partner in a global law firm and loving father of twins with his partner Monique.

CHAPTER

Four

*The freedom to be able to
dream (and live your dream)*

In the years' 1997-2006, for almost 10 years I worked as an employee. I worked for 5 different companies and looking back, I have made some important observations that I did not realize, and I was not consciously aware of at that time, at that age (24 – 33 years old).

First the story:

The first job was for a food retailer. I worked my way up from discovering, knowing, improving, and working in every department of their stores to become a store manager in just 2 years of time. I loved working there. Basic but intelligent company, down to earth, a lot of learning possibilities, teamwork, both physically and mentally challenging job. My lovely wife and I bought an old farmer's house in January 1999 to renew and live in. At the same time, I got a job offer (I was not actively searching) with a pay rise, company car, etc. and decided to leave the retail company and start a new adventure. The salary in food retail was not great, it involved long hours and a 6-day work week but I loved the job and working with the people. So why change?

This new job as a key account manager for a drinks

manufacturer only lasted a few months. My job was to negotiate with Food Retailers to list our products, work out promotional campaigns and get good placement for our products in the stores. I really learned a lot in a very short period of time. The second month I held this job, my wife saw in the newspaper that a Petrol company was hiring somebody to help manage their stores of the Gas stations. She "thought" that it could be something for me... I promised my darling I would do one interview (what harm could it do?), I got the job and started at this massive international petrol company, where everybody worked for "Oil or derived oil products", except for a few young cowboys in the "Non-Fuel" team. Remarkable job title that was...a non-job ☺. Why did this change happen?

I worked in this petrol company for 5 fantastic years with great results, 2 fusions with other petrol companies, a growing market share that in the meanwhile meant working for the market leader in our country. Putting in a lot of hours and many, many kilometers on the road away from home but very well paid, great advantages and lots of holiday days. A job and company for a lifetime you would say, as were my thoughts. "I will build my career here". But ... you feel it coming, events happened. A phone call came from a person I knew who asked me to come with him, work for him in a very interesting and challenging adventure...

I took the leap and started working for this wholesale company with very low % gross margin but very high turnover. Our objective was to make the % gross margin grow with 0,1-0,2 points. On a massive turnover, a huge amount of money. We were really well on the way after just 10 months of aligning suppliers, internal & external sales team, the buying division, tech division etc. until.... my person of trust (the general manager) was sacked out of the blue one day. Since I was his pupil, I sensed what was going to happen the next days. How was I going to tell this at home? 2 children, a third on the way, a heavy mortgage and just, according to all my family and friends, foolishly left a fantastic job, at the petrol company, for a crazy adventure...

That same week out of nowhere again a phone call came. A competitor petrol company had heard I left the market leader and wanted to know if I was up for a meeting, just to talk and get to know each other... Why did these things happen and why did that very important lifeline come?

Starting bright and early every morning in the new job, again at a petrol company, putting on the lights in their big offices in the morning and turning them off in the evening. Although loving the job, loving the content of the job for a smaller market player, a challenger, loving the team-work, the benefits and package I became more and more aware of a feeling that became stronger and stronger... but I did not know why, what, how.

In 2006 after one year working for this challenger petrol company, I met someone, a supplier who, like the general manager at my previous job, was self-employed. He ran his own company, very motivated. I learned from our long talks that he was sometimes very troubled and challenged and worried but on the other hand inspired and visionary and exciting.

I was then and there, early 2006 I started understanding my feeling that became stronger and stronger and made me decide the steps I took...

So far, the short version of the story of these 10 interesting years. I would love to tell you more about my family's and my learnings & challenges, successes and goals during this period but that is for the next time.

Now for the observations I made, the why behind the events and the understanding of that feeling that was getting stronger and stronger. And the results and outcome.

I strongly believe and see proof in my personal story that my natural actions and positive behavior and unconscious and positive life philosophy played a very big role in the events that happened and "the luck" I had.

Coincidence does not exist. The phone calls that came, the hints and ideas from other people like my wife's are a result of who you are, what you do and especially who you are and what you do to and for other people and even more how you make them feel.

I learnt I am a competitive person, wanting to succeed. I have a temper when things do not go the way I plan. On the other hand, I also want others to succeed and be happy. I need people around me who love what they do and do what they love.

I learnt that people saw me as a very confident person, who exactly knows what he wants and knows where he is going. He is always in for a laugh and shares joy, but serious when needed. They saw me as successful and exemplary and a bit of a rebel. Yes, I have talents and yes, I am passionate and I work hard.

But in fact, I often felt very unsure inside. I was kind and very positive to everyone because I am like that but also because I did not want to upset anyone or hurt them or because I was afraid, they would be mad at me or that they would not like me. I was raised to be very respectful to seniors and more experienced people and did not see myself as a rebel, on the contrary when people show you the mirror of how they see you, you become aware that some things are very different from how you are and feel yourself from within.

So, since then I have been working on knowing myself and understanding myself every single day. I work and study on learning and understanding how other people function, think and act and how to interpret that and communicate better. How does our brain, our most important tool work and how can you use that to the benefit of everyone?

I also learned to express how I feel and not only what I think openly. Opening up to others around you in a very sincere and honest way builds respect, builds trust. Do not be afraid to be vulnerable. Opening up often turns one of your weaknesses into strength because you are now more aware of it yourself and you will start working on it.

Knowing your strengths, challenges and weaknesses is important but using your strengths to the best of everyone, facing your challenges and working on your weaknesses and not ignoring them is the next and indispensable step. This step for me took away so much uncertainty that I now can say that people who see me as very confident are right.

Coming back to this deeper lying feeling. I grew

up in a family with two elder brothers, my mother was a nurse, and my father was a teacher. I was born, three years younger than the second brother. Although he was sick and my parents knew there was a risk, my mother's Christian faith led to my birth.

Thus, I was raised in a very protective environment. Nothing was to happen to me, one child with a handicap in our family, our home led to an atmosphere of fear towards a lot of things. No friends that were not approved of, no playing outside on the streets. I am not saying I was an unhappy child, but it felt a bit like a glass palace. As a teenager I would have loved to ride a motorcycle and go out to parties. I did do a lot of sports, something I still very much enjoy.

You can imagine that when, at the age of 17 or 18, I decided to leave the nest, move out and find a job and go to study, a whole new world opened up to me. New friends, many friends, falling and getting up again, organizing student events, discovering all that knowledge and life had to offer.

For the first time in my life, I was held responsible for my own choices. But I could also make my own plans, think about my future. Often people say that their time as a student is the most beautiful time of their life. It is because you discover the world, learn to be accountable, very much enjoy life and friends and girlfriends, but you do not carry responsibilities of a family, your job and taking care of others yet. I met my wife during those years and we still have many friends from those wonderful years.

What does this have to do with that deeper lying feeling that became stronger and stronger?

After the ten interesting years as an employee, as a new husband and a young father I decided in 2006 to start my own company. I was intrigued by the other business owners I met and carried by that strong feeling that made me leave home at the age of 17 or 18, that feeling that made me change jobs in search of something new and that feeling that became completely clear and present when I started building my families' own future as a business starter.

This feeling in fact is not a feeling, it is the freedom to be able to dream and live your dream while you learn to listen, learn and appreciate. It is taking the high road, the long road and making choices at the crossroads, all at the same time, but most of all for me it is to live a life to serve others.

Surely in your life you have met people, seen people spoken and performed, worked with people and you said to yourself, wow, they are so good, they are so brave, they are so strong. It is my strong conviction and belief, no in fact I know that these people got to that stage of wowing others because they discovered their talents and reinforced them, they knew their weaknesses and they turned them into strengths. But if next to that wow effect when you see them move and speak to you and others, you also feel that other thing, that thing we would say: he/she is special. It is because they have the spirit, they have found that special place where they experience the freedom to be able to dream.

Of course, that person can be very beautiful and especially talented at what he/she does, but that extra sparkle is not because of being handsome or very good, it is because they are very beautiful inside and at peace with themselves, they dream and live the dream, they live to serve others, they approach every day as a gift and every situation from a positive attitude.

It is not the end point, the realization of your goals or dreams that makes you happy when you reach them, it is the road towards it. Living the dream of being free to be able to dream and serve others that will make you experience true happiness and of course love.

My wife, Annelies and I have known each other for 26 years now. Our four boys are at the ages of 9, 14, 16 and

18. We have three businesses. It has been a challenging road and it still is and will be. Yet, we live each day to dream, to learn and help others.

Eight years ago, I called up Pierre Schmitt, now a very good and dear business friend, and made an appointment with him to meet and see each other for the first time on a business fare. We connected. He invited me into a business community that exactly represents all of my thoughts and beliefs I wrote above. This network of entrepreneurs is called BNI, Business Network International, and it brings together like minded businesspeople all starting from the beautiful philosophy of Givers Gain. How "lucky" I was again to be introduced in this community that again changed our lives for the better, helped us grow further as persons whilst the image of our dream still becomes clearer and clearer.

Last thing I really want to share with you is my credo: Train hard, Race Hard, Party Hard, Adapt and Repeat. As I told you before, I always did some sports. I have been training for triathlons now since 2012 and I am very proud I have finished in two full distance Triathlons. 3.8 km of swimming, 180.2 km of biking and 42,195 km of running (the marathon). Finishing this kind of races is a very emotional moment and very fulfilling. But also, here the road towards the race, all the weeks and months of hard hours of training, looking after your nutrition is really the important part. I would advise everyone to do physical exercise. Walking, swimming, biking, no matter what kind of exercise because if you do it regularly you will feel your body improve, your mind will work better, you will sleep better. It is however important that you do the exercise with the right material and intensity. I personally get my best ideas and best clear insights on situations while exercising.

My credo is not only valid for my sports. I train hard, work hard, study and read a lot also in business and family life. I race hard, make sure that when I do the job, work for the client, do things with your family that I am there in that moment, not distracted by anything else and give it everything and more. Party hard: successes as well as learnings must be celebrated! You can reward yourself or share the party with others but celebrate! It does not always have to be a big party even small things, small rewards given and received are equally important. And then evaluate, adapt according to your learnings if necessary and repeat the success formula over and over again.

It would make me feel very happy if, with this, I can help you, dear reader, find the freedom to be able to dream. Please don't forget: live the dream by taking the paths and roads ahead, trusting on your choices, hard work, skills, learnings and trusting the people around you that you serve, love, accept, care for and help them feel and find the freedom as well.

About Jan De Wachter

Jan De Wachter (1973) grew up in a family with two older brothers in a very small town in the Flemish speaking part of Belgium.

He has a master-in-Economics degree (1996, University of Leuven in Belgium) with specialty in International and Monetary economics and Econometry. During his studies 26 years ago, he met his wife Annelies.

They have been married for 19 years now and they have four children between 10 and 18 years old, all boys.

His professional career started in Retail sector; there he worked for big National and International brands. He developed his further management, team and people skills in the Petrol Sector working for companies like Total and Q8. In 2006 he became a self-employed Retail Consultant and soon co-owner in several companies in different activities. Through his business relationship with Pierre Schmitt (ED in Flemish Belgium), Jan became a BNI member in January 2013 and a few months later he started as a Regional Director his own BNI region from 0. Since March 2014 Jan has been the Executive Director of this region (called BNI Limburg) that now counts 17 chapters, +400 members and most of all a proud BNI Team of 1 SDC, 10 DC's and +20 Ambassadors.

He is a member of BNI's Founder's Circle and was elected by his peers to be the Vice President of this Founder's Circle for the next two years.

His time away from business he loves to spend it with his wife and kids on skiing or camper holidays or on weekends with friends. He is a dedicated Triathlete. He is a finisher in 2 full distance Iron Man Triathlons and several marathons.

Connecting people, inspiring them and seeing them grow gives him the biggest satisfaction.

What nobody knows about him: from the age of 6 he was on stage for recitation and diction contests. His secret to success: surrounding myself with good people to accomplish the things I cannot do alone and achieve the goals I couldn't imagine even possible.

CHAPTER

Five

19 Middleton Road

"An INVESTMENT in knowledge pays the best Interest."

– Benjamin Franklin

The beginnings of my journey into entrepreneurship ......

Is it when my grandfather made me sweep the front driveway of 19 Middleton Road, Golders Green, London? Remembering the conditions as a 6-year-old on a sunny windy autumn day? The driveway required constant sweeping to get the Autumn leaves into hessian bags for removal by the gardener. The leaves were all swelling up in small mounds across the driveway. The large leaves rustling around in the wind. Using two cut out sides from a cardboard box to trap and scoop the leaves in piles and with a broom taller than me. The piles constantly moving and the ever-elusive leaf that never manages to make its way into the hessian bags. Its flight capturing for that moment as it flies over the rooftops. These formative, single digit years, those experiences, the smells, and sights and the sounds. The recollections of the words of advice on life, investment, trust, loyalty came directly from my grandparents and parents. My grandfather was always giving me words of wisdom, on that that day in the driveway, he delivered "doesn't matter what you do Mark, so long as you do it well!".

My childhood began in North London, before migrating to Perth, Western Australia, at the age of nine. I undertook all my formative school years and subsequent university years in Perth. Long hot summers became the norm, swimming, surfing, and surviving became my teenage years. My parents endured countless occasions on my behalf where there wasn't entrepreneurial mindset present, just plain stupidity on my behalf. These formative experiences appear as milestones and growth opportunities today. Is it that entrepreneurs learn more from getting things wrong than right ?

My entry into true entrepreneurship probably came via babysitting. The local neighbours and friends' children were my first jobs at fourteen, and then as I got multiple jobs, I needed to deploy others (my first entry into recruitment). Namely these were my sisters and my sisters' friends, as demand increased and as I moved up the pay per hour scale.

My mother ran a highly successful kosher catering business within the community for over twenty years. As I reached fifteen, my exposure to business, customer service, preparation, timeliness, staffing, and being the owner's son soon gave me some very precious lifelong learning experiences. Many hours on standing on my feet. The chance to work with friends constantly and the access to food!

These were amazing years in recollection, teamwork, working for one another. The real life understanding of being prepared, looking after vital equipment. All pillars that still present themselves today in a variety of forms and decisions.

My father was a mechanical engineer from the UK, he was always trading and up scaling motor vehicles, from his early years living in London. His car obsession in his youth continued onwards as he became a husband and then father. We imported several cars during our time in Australia. I loved the cars we had. Large bucket leather seats in Jaguars, wooden dashboards, smooth lines. I was privileged in my role allocation Dad gave me. It was the coveted role of chief polisher and tyre cleaner ! Least possible damage ! That's it. However, the Jaguar Mark 4, XJ20 V12, Panther SS100 and Austin Healey's all were revamped, rejuvenated, re-engineered and unfortunately sold before the racing car driver's son got his hands behind a wheel. Yeah ! My Dad was a racing car driver (part-time) and won several coveted speed trials and Races at Brands Hatch Circuit, UK. Holding the record for spinning an old Ford Anglia twelve times ! I only ever sat in the driver's seat while the vehicles were stationary, imagining the time when I would get to drive cars like this. Thinking it was my entitlement and rite of passage. Obviously, Dad thought otherwise ! Lesson learnt, do not assume !

Those were wonderful times, learning about cars, collecting model cars. The process from start to finish of car construction, the designs, name classifications, and engineering geometry of it, all was fascinating. I remember as a boy meeting Stirling Moss, the famous racing driver, and taking photos, watching the support team around him. I was dragged endlessly, through many car mechanics workshops, fabrication workshops, racing tracks, and loads of tyre shops during my early years in the UK. Travelling with dad, adventures, research and watching him interact with all sorts of people, from all cultures and countries. His grace with people and making them feel comfortable around him still guides me to this day. His racing passion stopped when we arrived in Australia, and with a growing family, living in a new country, it was not his passion anymore. The car modifications slowed, as Australian sales excise tariffs rose, and custom duties started to become more significant. So, we traded Australian made vehicles instead, mainly Holden's and Ford's, with ample supply of parts and wreckers' yards. My father had another secret weapon, my mother would often say obsession, and it was not so secret. His stamp collection from of over 70 years. This was also combined with his amazing Model Car Collection. The stamps gave me so much learning, a window to the world, fascinating destinations, new words and places.

It was incredible learning, as I look back now, some forty years on. The model cars were play toys to me then, over time they have now become investments. The stamps showed me, attention to detail, organisation, categorisation, recording, storing, presenting, pricing, auctions, all a complete specialised language existing within a sub-culture of collectors/enthusiasts at a serious philatelist level, and then my father! We lived with stamps everywhere, he was always at auctions, stamp shows, packages arriving and presenting on topics through the window of his stamps. This was well before we had the ease of Power Point ! All his presentation sheets were prepared on a typewriter. Topics such as Great White Sharks, Monotrenes (Playtpus), Tristan De Cuba (Island), Ferrari's, Jaguars, Racing Tracks, Racing Car Drivers, Formula 1, anything Fangio and his Israeli Collection was the jealousy of many world philatelists and investors ! I still remember the constant soaking of stamps on paper towels nightly by the kettle, soaking off the used stamps. The main rule: No water jugs or anything fluid in his office – Ever ! Children, drinks, and mint sheets of expensive stamps don't mix !

So, with a mixture of tyre polish and smoked salmon bagels, my two senses of taste and touch began in all earnest. I really began to make a significant pathway towards being a serial entrepreneur and master connector once I graduated. A Bachelor's Degree in Education majoring in Mathematics, from Edith Cowan University, WA. During my university years, or what my mother described as my surfing and windsurfing years, I was tutoring high school students on weekday afternoons during school terms. It was extremely lucrative and easy money. I loved the premise that I collected a large sum at the end of each term. The big pay-out! You worked hard and didn't have the temptation of immediate spending. Tutoring was mainly weekday afternoons after school hours. Driving to a variety of homes on a per hour charge basis. This started increasing and demand exceeded the hours available. I started to use the weekends, especially Saturday mornings as another prime tutoring timeslot. I built up a considerable client base and was now giving several other maths-teaching colleagues my overflow. However, this business would have to wait. Europe and London were calling.

After having taught mathematics in various schools and systems across Perth, combined with my love for surfing and windsurfing for a duration of three years, eventually the roots in the UK called. Thus, the real entry into entrepreneurship began at a whole different level. I lived with my grandmother Alice Graber, at 19 Middleton Road, Golders Green, two streets away from the beautiful and tranquil Hampstead Heath in North London. It was an amazing time, teaching relief at various schools within Inner London, some permanent term placements and opening my eyes to everything international!

My grandparents' house in Golders Green had four levels, the cellar, the lowest below ground level was used as a bomb shelter in the second world war, now it is a gardeners storage shed, it consisted of generations of boxes, with can't throw away items. The three levels above the cellar consisted of bedrooms, toilets, bathrooms. The top level had two bedrooms, one of which became mine and the opposite bedroom subsequently became my study/office. During the second world war my grandpa Sam was an Air Warden in North London and this is where he would raise the alarm as the German's bombed London, looking out across the rooftops from my bedroom window I recall the view, and the frightening feeling and sounds my grandfather would have observed.

The ground level was the formal entertaining, living rooms and extensive kitchen and outdoor raised patio. I loved those summer afternoons, and Grandma would have tea ready for me after teaching at school. I would ride my bike back over the Hampstead Heath returning to 19 Middleton Road and arrive to sit on the outdoor patio with tea served on a tea cart filled with digestive biscuits and chocolates. Listening to my grandmother's words of wisdom and life stories. Funny how when two distinct senses are heightened: sight and taste, and how the memories are stronger and remain longer. The beautiful lush green garden below to gaze my eyes over as I sipped hot well brewed tea in a "china" cup, dipping my penguin biscuits. It's the small things in life.

I began my Master's in Education at London University, subsequently completing that in conjunction with units studied at the University of Western Australia. I went on and taught at private boys schools and single-sex comprehensive schools within Inner London, for close to five years consecutively. I truly learnt the value of my Australian education and qualifications, mathematics teaching work was plentiful, and I had free board, lodgings, and love.

I made several lifelong relationships during this time, but in particular, this person, who will remain anonymous, opened my eyes to so much during this crucial period of my life. I will be forever thankful that our two worlds collided 35 years ago, and we still continue to have many collisions to this day. From this amazing friendship, fellowship, and partnership, came forth my introduction into the world of importation, memorandums of understanding, international bank currency exchange and of course commercial lawyers. Truly building an international network had begun. We imported beer from Canadian Breweries and sold it into the "Dollar Shops", as they were then called. These were former Soviet Union countries, that were now openly selling western goods for American Currency. We procured and distributed several shipping containers of beer to these eastern European destinations. It gave me insight into Marketing, Management and Logistics in real time.

The ability to work in Europe gave me further perspective to my roots in Western Australia, the United Kingdom fits into WA 14 times ! The UK has a population above 65 million people, WA close to 2 million mainly situated in and around its capital city, Perth. 80% of Australians live on the coast. Europe was vastly different, no matter how many times I was asked to compare the two. I never could, both worlds so vastly different. Both with their individual personalities and cultures, each location having its unique calling.

So, after five years away, I returned home to Perth. How I had missed the early beach mornings, the crunch of fresh sand, the salt water. The feel of my wetsuit Hugging to me in the cold autumn waters. But, most important, the space and the freedom to think.

Teaching, tutoring all things, mathematics education was extremely fruitful upon my return. I began venturing further forward in business and took the opportunity of doing group matriculation (Year 12) pre-examination workshops. I was appointed a role as lead examiner for over ten years in the preparation and creation of several Final Matriculation Examination Papers that were sat by all students in the state. This also meant the preparation and presentation of marking guideline workshops to the 100 plus employed markers (mathematics teachers) by the state education department, who graded each individual script then compared results to their appointed co-marker. This experience connected me with other like-minded Mathematics Teachers (external tutors) who were also applying this to their tutoring craft undoubtedly, gaining valuable insight, and higher charges.

Graber Mathematics, my tutoring business began, we started targeting holiday periods, weekend pre-examination workshops, pre-school year warm up sessions, etc. With the extensive matriculation examination experience, the Final Year 12 market created much greater price flexibility and allowed us to increase the charges for Year 12 sessions. Discounts for sets of sessions, loyalty cards, and then increased charges for one off "cram" session. The emergence of being at the right place and right time again. Now, with the introduction of graphic calculators into the Western Australian curriculum this was timely. This poised well and we created additional student tutoring sessions, for purely graphic calculators to increase efficiency and further value add.

All this meant multiple students, more multiple/ group sessions, and higher per hour charges, together with a now incurred venue charge. This venture became extremely successful, where much like my babysitting lessons, I began recruiting other mathematics teachers to support the demand. Graber Mathematics was well and truly launched. It catered for after school groups or individual sessions, and we had a secured premise that was positioned strategically between the most clustered private schools. My early entry into logistics yet again became beneficial. Soon, it became clear that this substantial business was achieving far greater income than a year's salary as a teacher. However, doing both, represented the best decision for me at that stage and time in my life. I was however totally time poor and not really enjoying the benefits of my work and sacrifice of time. Graber Mathematics exceeded all expectations and allowed me significant visibility and credibility within the education sector. It became a logical step to create private, VIP students who requested ONLY me ! I was awarded

Life Membership of the WA Mathematics Association for my contribution to Mathematics education in WA. The owner and founder of a successful tutoring business. Still teaching full-time. House Master at a Private Boys school. You could say, "I needed to make some decisions!". Graber Mathematics with little or no competition in the retail market, apart from Kumon, at the time was prime to be sold. With competition mainly from private mathematics teachers, who could never handle the volume or outgoings that Graber Mathematics secured, the answer became obvious. Sell the business !

The VIP tutoring from my private home office was giving me far more significant resources and allowed me yet again time to pivot and strategize. I sold Graber Mathematics with 300 students, who were in regular tutoring programs to a husband and wife maths teacher team and the business still runs today under another name. I then began to create the start of my next venture WebSmart Design.

★ ★ ★ ★ ★ ★ ★ ★ ★ ★

About Mark Graber

Mark Graber Mathematics Teacher, Senior Lecturer, BNI Franchise Owner, Certified LEGO Facilitator. He hails from Perth, Western Australia, where he spent 15 years as a high school mathematics teacher and over 10 years as a senior lecturer at Curtin Business School. Within BNI, Mark is an Executive Director across four regions in British Columbia, Canada.

As a passionate educator through and through, he brings his ability to engage groups and teams to move past what seems impossible - into success.

Mark Graber has been involved with BNI for over sixteen years. He has seen the organisation move through various strategic and organisational changes. Mark has come through his own passage in BNI, from being a chapter member to an Executive Director, with significant professional and personal learning development. He has contributed and created innovations that have been taken on globally.

Mark has a flair for collaborative work and team cohesion, this has been extremely beneficial within his journey in BNI. The passing of BNI knowledge from generation to generation has been particularly enjoyable for Mark. He lives and breathes the "givers gain" philosophy. His passion for education has always been paramount to him.

Mark is most passionate about "what the future holds", he is extremely passionate about the education of business professionals.

Mark currently sits on the BNI Global Innovation Task Force that helps guides 275000+ members globally. Mark spent over ten years as a senior lecturer at Curtin Business School, and this has enhanced his ability to apply knowledge within a business context.

"Within BNI we have the ability to impact hundreds of thousands of BNI members and their families."

This legacy of "making a difference" has always been a lifetime goal for Mark!

As a professional speaker, Mark is regularly asked to speak on the subjects of referral marketing, personal leadership, business leadership, mathematics and LEGO.

CHAPTER
Six

Establishing 10 own businesses

"Establishing 10 own businesses" that was my career aspiration when i got my high school diploma in 1992. The problem was that I had no idea what a promising way will be to establish them. There is no place to learn how to establish a business. The motivation was to leave a footprint. I wanted to see if I could be successful in my own business and if I could create jobs for people. And one of the most important reasons was that I am a rebel and I hate to be told what to do. I need the feeling to do something significant for people and to help them. So, I needed to be my own boss. I felt too young and too inexperienced to start my own business and the way to find my dream job was not defined.

I wanted to be a stockbroker at the Frankfurt Stock Exchange. But this job was limited to few brokers and nobody could tell me how to get there. School did not prepare me for this journey. I decided to start with an avocational training in a credit institution (Stadt Sparkasse Solingen). I wanted to learn more about investing money, credits, stocks, and the way money works. In the last months of the avocational training, they wanted me to start selling products to the customers. Many of the products had no customer benefits!

I decided to sell only products the customers needed. As you can imagine, I had some discussions with my bosses about that issue. The day my contract ended, and I got my education certificate, I quitted the job. After having finished the training, I decided to study economics at the University of Cologne to deepen my skills and learn some new ones. At that time, at University, I did a lot of training on the job in different companies. For example, I worked for Johnson Controls headquarter Europe in the Marketing, HR and Controlling department for practical application, and as to theoretic knowledge I learned from my Professors. Then, I worked for a consulting company besides studying. By analyzing other companies, I hoped to learn how to run my own business. I thought I would have learnt a lot and that it would have helped me to start my first business. I got some good basis that helped me in some small parts you need as a business owner; the job trainings gave me some ideas of the way bigger companies are organized.

I learned that school and even university just teach you things you need as an employee. They make you an expert in one job, but being an entrepreneur means that you must handle many jobs in one person. The more I learned I felt I had to start something of my own. I would only learn the important things if it were mine. I remembered my wish to be a stockbroker and so I chose a job that was like it. I started as financial advisor for a big multilevel marketing company named "Tecis" in form of an independent sales representative. They gave me a lot of trainings as to different aspects of the job. All kinds of insurances, investment funds, stocks, credits, properties, private equity and many more. But also, in recruitment of new partners, selling psychology, DISC analysis. I loved it because it felt real and I had practical use of it. I asked a lot of questions and tried to learn as much as I could. I worked 14 to 16 hours a day not only to understand the product side but also the business side. I looked deep in the business plan, the career plan, and the compensation plan Tecis had given us. I compared and analyzed our products to the other products on the market. That took me one year. In this year I recruited some new advisors in my team, I became a team leader and developed some personal skills in leading and teaching people. Some colleagues became good friends and we decided we could do both a better business plan, career plan and a compensation plan and that we could build a better company. I felt ready for that! I finished University very quickly in order to invest 100% of my time for the new company. We did it. We started our own company named "Solut financial consulting AG". We grew amazingly fast up to more than 100 independent financial advisors at several locations in West Germany.

If I could step back in time, what would I tell my younger advisors how to start as an entrepreneur?

1. Have a clear "Why" for yourself

The first years as an entrepreneur are extremely exciting but also very hard! You will have to work many hours and if you earn some money you will have to invest it back in your business. Sometimes you will succeed and sometimes you will fail. You will try and make errors. To go along this path, you need a strong support from your partner in life, your friends and family. You need a strong "why" to build your own company. Only with a strong belief in your why and yourself you will master the challenges of the first years. Write down your why, talk about it with your family and friends. Try to get it really deep. You will need it!

We started our first company "Solut financial consulting AG" with a bunch of 5 friends. We built the business plan, the business corporations to the investment and insurance companies, the compensation plan, the CI/CD, our brand name and much more. At that time, we earned no money because we had to build a system and the complete background for the company and we had no time to sell products. It was important to talk and think about our why! We wanted to build the perfect place for financial advisors, for us. We knew it would have been very hard in the first months or years without big checks! We were taking a high risk. There were many people who could not understand why we were taking those risks, we all could have good paid jobs in other companies. Some of our girlfriends and parents did. We had no investors, only our small money we had earned as students. It was hard to sign a 5-year contract for our office when we just had money for 6 months. And it took time to organize all the things we needed for a running system. Without a strong why we would have been knocked down by some of the setbacks that happened at the beginning. For example, we were not allowed to take our customer from the old company with us. The marketing costs for the launch and branding were much higher than we had expected. The commissions we could negotiate with our product partners were lower than expected, and only got higher with the volume we made with their products. There were enough situations to give up, but we had a strong why and believed in our business model. That's why we rented big business premises because we wanted to expand fast and find new advisors. That and our enthusiasm made us attractive for new advisors. That is why you need a strong why to start your business. You must take risks, others will not understand the way you go, you will fail over and over again. But finally, you will make it and you will feel damn well.

2. Learn

If you know what kind of business you will launch, think about what you need to know to make it successful. Then figure out where you can learn the professional skills you need. May be at university, avocational training, or internships. If you do that in advance, it can save you a lot of money and time. Warning! Those professional skills are perfect for employees and self-employed people but are far not enough for a business owner. It is not only the professional skills you need. As a business owner you must be multi-talented! Normally, you will start alone, and all departments of a company will be in one person. You need a strong mindset and believe in what you are doing. You need skills in accounting to understand the numbers of your company. You need skills in law to understand the contracts you enter into, the terms and conditions, and data protection. You need skills in human resources and social insurance when you employ people. You need marketing skills to represent your company and many more skills to run a successful business. When your business grows you can employ experts for those jobs in your company.

3. Sales is one of the most important skills for an Entrepreneur

Most importantly, you need very good skills in sales

and negotiation, that is quite similar for me too.

There are so many great specialists out there, but if you cannot sell your products or services to the customers, it is absolutely worthless, and you will fail. It does not matter what your business is, you always must sell! It might be the products or services for your customers, but also your business idea to the banker or investors to get money. You must sell the business model to suppliers, to budding employees, to your friends because they will not see you as much as before. I heard so many people telling me "I am a consultant, I do not sell", this is a bad thing. Even a consultant must sell his services and acquire new clients. I met many people that wanted to take a shortcut because they did not like to get no´s. "I like selling, but I have to learn it". We will not be successful without skills in selling. Learn to love it. Look for jobs where you can learn selling. When my kids were in the kinder garden, they sold waffles in a hardware store. They had a waffle stand at a specific place and when I arrived, some parents with th kids were standing there and waiting for customers. I took about 20 waffles to some kids and went through the market to talk to the people in the store. The price was 1 € for each waffle. When they asked me for the price, I told them 1 € each, but it would have been great for the kids if they were willing to give more. The kids loved it and they did the same. Some of the parents felt ashamed about the way we did it. But we sold our 20 waffles in a few minutes and the parents at the stand 20 in maybe one hour. For me it is the best feeling to make a great deal! Sometimes it is a good deal in purchasing and sometimes in sales. The most money you will make with those skills. The purchasing is particularly important, here you need good suppliers' analytics to get good prices. Then, it comes to the sales part. Many people even do not start selling, they try to bring all processes and the system to perfection before starting to sell. Entrepreneurship is a try and error process. Selling is a try and error process. The more no's you get will make you better and better. Try to get a lot of no's! Go for them. Do not let it get you. It is a game, so take it like a game. The best sportsmen are those that trained most, that means they have failed many more times than the others. For example, all great basketball players, like Michael Jordan or Kobe Bryant are in the top 10 ranking in missed shots! If you want to get very well in what you do, you must fail a lot. But try to make new mistakes and not the same repeatedly.

4. Teach others

The best way to learn is to teach. I always tried to get trainer in the organizations I was. In our Financial Advisor Business, I was a training manager. By this job,

I had to be very good on the product side and on the sales side. I put pressure on myself with that job. I wanted to be sure to be able to answer any questions our advisors could have. And even the questions I could not answer helped me to get better, because I had to find the right answers. That made me strong in my own customer meetings. Training Customer consultations was also to my advantage. By teaching them and spending a lot of time in trainings I got very self-confident. I learned from the mistakes of the advisors in the trainings. I learned by developing new pictures and ideas to explain the products to the customers. I learned by exchange of experience with the team about their results on the field. Work in teams, a group of people is smarter than a single person.

5. Personal development/growth

Never stop to get better! Look for good coaches, business angels and experienced entrepreneurs you can learn from and who can guide you. It is good to double check new ideas with other business owners. They can give you different views on your topics. Do exchange of experience with those people. You can learn from each other. You can pick the best of them and implement them. Talk to businesspeople in your industry, who are successful. Watch your biggest competitor and learn how he got successful. To copy success is a smart thing.

When your business is running, start thinking out of the box. Talk to businesspeople from other industries and learn from them. May be there are successful things that are unusual in your branch. Try those things if they work in your branch too. For example, I learned from very experienced and successful network marketers how to invite a huge crowd of people for a business presentation. I did the same procedure to invite people for my financial advisor business. I had never heard before that a company from the financial industry had ever done it, but it was a great event and we had great success with that event. Never stop personal growth.

6. Challenge yourself

If there is a challenge or an opportunity you feel uncomfortable, take it. Go out of your comfort zone. That is the place where you will find success. I have a funny story for you. I feel very uncomfortable on a stage. I am introverted. I had to learn it in a very hard way. I signed in for a talent song contest with more than 2000 people watching live. This contest was more a fun event. The most people going on stage lost bets and it was sure they would have embarrassed themselves. So, did I. I am a horrible singer, and my friends chose a horrible song for me. I was so nervous looking on all those people armed with eggs, tomatoes and water bombs. I was not afraid of those eggs and tomatoes! It was my fear to be on stage. My legs were shaking, my stomach had turned around and my voice was going to fail. It was horrible, but after that I had never problems again being on stage. A more business story of me. In my case, I hate social media, for me it is a waste of time and I privately will never use it. But for my business it could be a huge impact. So, I booked some social media courses and coaches to get more experienced in that special part of marketing. And I employed a young man who had studied social media marketing, because I did not need to be an expert in it but I had to learn what it could be for my business. If you do it, do it 100%. That led me to my last advice.

7. Start fast and go all in

You need a strong momentum at the beginning. Do not hesitate. To grow a business takes time, but if you do it part time it will last awfully long. Cut of the secure line and give 100% for your new business. Like the old conquerors who burned down their sips when they reached land. There was only one chance for them. They had to win! They could not flee and run home! And that is the way you will be successful, you must. Your strong why will help you to start fast and reach the first steps to your final goal. Only if you burn inside for your business you will be able to set people on fire for your business, services, and products. Do not try to push many things at the same time. Start and go all in.

For example, when I decided to build a big team in my financial advisor business, I planned how I would have done it. I stopped all activities that were not necessary for life. I made a list of activities I could do and a list of people I would have invited. I scheduled my activities and I started to invite people and started all activities. After a month I had 11 new advisors in my team, while the other leaders in our organization where still planning or doing it step by step. They called maybe 1 or 2 person a day. I called 50! The example above with the social media was the same. When I decided that I wanted to implement social media marketing, I invested money and time. I wanted to have the first sales in 8 weeks. I also could have invested 1 hour a week at the weekend to watch a free YouTube video about social media marketing and then maybe in 3 month there would have been a workshop I could have participated. But that would have lasted too long. Start fast and go all in. That will lead you to a faster success and you can focus the next challenge in your company.

About Markus Bosdorf

Markus has started several companies on his own or with partners. His first business was in the financial advisor industry, followed by several companies in the consulting, training and sales industry.

He has been a trainer in sports (tennis, team handball, fitness). In the companies he founded or was involved, he trained skills like sales, recruiting and motivation.

Currently, he is

- Executive Director of BNI NRW in Germany with 2 partners. In BNI he is national trainer and member of the founder circle.
- Professional Amazon reseller.
- Managing Director of a software development company, which develops and distributes its own products.
- Managing Director of a business lounge.
- Co-Founder of a Mobile App (Mindzip and Citagram)

PERSONAL INFORMATION:

He is a fan of lifelong learning and is a webinar junkie. He is particularly interested in personal growth, sales, leadership, crypto currencies, economics and environmental protection.

Markus loves traveling to foreign countries and connecting to people and different cultures. He loves the nature, sea, and mountains.

He likes concerts, and sport events. He would like to visit the Olympic games.

HIS PROFESSIONAL DESIRE IS TO find a project that makes the difference for the world in a positive way.

CHAPTER

Seven

*The Efficiency Machine,
The Potential, The Restart, and
The Wise Man*

An Efficiency Machine.

That was the vision given to me by most teachers in the University of what I should become when I started working and what we should expect from others as well – that was the worst part.

That line of thinking led me to experience some negative situations that could have been avoided if I were taught differently. Also, my professional life would have been a lot easier, especially in the parts where I had to deal with other people – that is almost always.

I remember that in my early professional days, I started working in the largest supermarket company in my country as a Financial Assistant, and my Division Manager asked me to create a new type of report, connecting many areas of my department. He told me to go to another building and talk to a session supervisor called Eduardo, that he would have had at least half of the data I needed.

Having the only efficiency in my mind, I walked into his office already asking for the data; he interrupted me - with a not so happy face - and said:

- "Hi, good morning, I am Eduardo; we haven't met before; who are you?".

That answer really bothered me; I was in a hurry to create the report.

- "I am Paulo. Do you have this data?" I replied.

- "And which division are you from?" Eduardo went on, not making it easy for me.

- "Credit, I am the General Manager's Assessor, and he told me to create a report and ask you for the data." I hoped that answer would give me what I needed.

- "OK, Paulo, and what makes you think you can walk into my office, demanding internal data, without even presenting yourself? If you want anything from anyone in your work environment, you must first know them, and they need to know who you are; I can give you the data, but if you and I become good colleagues, I may even help you with your report."

- I was immediately, completely, taken out of my 100% Efficiency Machine mindset and thrown straight into reality. Eduardo and I eventually became friends, and I thank him for that valuable lesson.

People are not machines, nor should they ever be treated like that. In the following years, I decided to change how I would have related to people at work and I would have become a lot more sociable. Quite a challenge, especially for an introvert with 100% focus on results, but it can be done, little by little.

Nowadays, I can make a presentation on a stage for 2000 people without any discomfort, but it still takes me a little while fitting in a new environment. The fact is, having developed people skills over time, things went a lot easier for me, like gathering information, having support in many ways, being "in the loop," being "heard" frequently, and with all that, improving my leadership skills.

The first step of becoming a good leader is that people in your team need to like you, and they will not if you don't care for them. You need to have people skills for that. When was the last time you sat with a colleague and talked about his family, passions, or problems? Did you offer help? Did you follow up to check if that situation was solved? Do this, show people around you that you have a legitimate interest in them, and you will see significant changes happen in your life because people will also start caring about you. Even your mood will get better, trust me!

We depend on people to grow and succeed; that can be interpreted in many ways. It really pains me when I see people saying things like "I am a self-made person!"

or "I succeeded by myself!" These people usually hit their chests with their hands while they say that – that is pure ego! Let's go back in time a little and reflect about this:

★ Did you have people in your life that nourished you, kept you warm and safe when you could not care for yourself? Did they teach you your first words?

★ Did you have teachers from whom you learned a language, math, history, geography, and many other important things?

★ Did you have friends that challenged you all the time? Did you have enemies that also taught you lessons?

★ Did you get growth opportunities from people above you in the organizational chart or learn important things from other colleagues in your professional career?

★ If you started your own business, did you really do it by yourself? Didn't you have to hire an accountant, get legal advice, and buy equipment created and produced by others? In the end, how good is a business if you do not have other people to buy from you?

★ Be opened to listening, to learning new things, changing the way you do things just because someone else had a better idea than yours, in short: be humble. Not a lamb, but a humble leader who values people and helps them grow, recognize their contributions publicly, generate results, and you will end up having a team that will do for you more than expected because you will also be doing that!

The Great Potential.

At some point, in the supermarket company, I ended up being transferred to the area I wanted since the beginning: marketing. After being there for a while, the whole credit division was extinct, and almost 3000 people lost their jobs. That was my first (of a few) economic recession as a working man.

I got the position of junior consultant in a Small Business and Marketing consulting company. My boss was not an easy person to deal with, but I really learned a lot from him. One day he called me to his room and said:

★ "Paulo, you have been with us for a couple of months, you are doing great work, and I can honestly say that you have great potential!"

★ "Thank you!" I said.

★ "No thanks! Let me remind you that potential is something that you are not, yet, and you will have to work really hard to become what I believe you can be. It is up to you to achieve that or not."

As I remember that day, a mix of feelings comes to me: on one hand, I was happy to listen to that, but on another, I really got shaken. I had already heard about my potential a couple of times before, but that was the first time that the message became clear: "I believe you can be great, but you're not yet."

I also believed in my potential, but what was I doing to achieve that? The answer is very little. The realization of that made me move forward, looking to improve myself in my areas of expertise and also in other areas, some of them not much related.

The danger of being someone considered to have potential is that it may lead to stagnation. Whenever I see someone around me in that situation, I try to pass what I learned. Sometimes it works, but, unfortunately, I see an increasing number of young people worrying more about appearances than reality.

I agree that it is not always enough to be good at something that people around you also need to notice that. The problem is that in some cases we notice around us a person, who has really nothing substantial to offer other than just some carefully chosen words, images, and a good presentation; at some point, people will realize that, and the earned respect may vanish as it never existed.

Do not fall into that trap. Study, learn, enrich yourself with knowledge, culture, create your own theories, and try to prove them, but more than that, also try to disprove them. When you have finished, you will have a solid knowledge base of ways to do and not to do things. Then, you can teach others and be respected, and that respect will endure.

Success using short cuts to this process will depend on luck to get things right the very first time. Luck is not knowledge, and one day you may not have it anymore. Are you willing to risk your image and credibility based on luck? It is your choice, but I advise you to take the right path to reach your full potential. I know I am still walking on mine because our potential expands the more knowledge we have!

The Restart.

An electronic engineer that is what I thought I would be in my life. So much that my High School also had a Technical Course in electronics. Thank God I did that because I simply hated it. I couldn't imagine myself following that career anymore.

I was lost, not knowing what to do next. I started seeking other professions, and it took me a while to figure out what I wanted. My family said I should be a lawyer, a scientist, or a dentist; my friends said I should be a doctor because I was usually first or second in Science Knowledge Marathons in school. I also loved personal computers so much that I used to study Operating Systems and other software manuals in my free time, just for fun.

Back then, I didn't want any of that as my profession. I wanted to be able to run companies and chose Business School, specializing in General Management and Marketing. It was a great choice, even though I didn't follow that career for too long.

There was a very strong economic recession in my country, not connected to any world recession but due to government economic measures. It was really hard to find jobs in my area, especially for someone who was starting his career. Being already married and with bills to pay, I had to do something about it.

With all my IT knowledge and lots of patience to teach, I started giving private lessons; in 3 months, I gained more money than ever before working in my area, but that was not also what I wanted for my life. I got a part-time job as a support technician in a large Internet Service Provider to have some stable income. Private teachers usually need to work for 9 months to get money for the whole year because few people keep having private lessons during vacations. After 4 months in that company,

I was promoted to supervisor due to my advanced IT knowledge and especially my business background. In 4 more months, I was the national coordinator, and that started to open many doors for me. Without noticing, what was supposed to be a temporary solution became a career, and the most important part, I loved it.

This whole story tells you that you need to seek knowledge in different areas to help you grow in an organization or have a steadier business of your own. Do not be a fanatic only studying the same specialty over and over; even though you may end up being technically great in something, that probably won't help you become a good leader, manager, director, or C Level professional, nor to have all necessary skills to conduct your business in the best way. Yes, someday you may hire professionals to help you, but when you are building your business from scratch, it may take a while for you to be able to do that.

A couple of years later, I started my own IT consulting company. We were successful for almost 17 years, until I decided to dedicate myself full time to another business that I was doing and was really passionate about; helping businesspeople getting more business. I decided to restart once again. The feeling was so great from doing it that I really wanted to develop it more and more.

Slowly I stopped renewing contracts with my IT clients so that I would not lose too much income while the other business grew. This restart was smooth compared to the first one.

Meanwhile, I had a lot to learn, new mentors to find, new theories to create and prove (and disprove), a new path to walk on that makes me happy while doing it; isn't that the whole point of it?

If you find a new passion, start working on it, not abandoning what you already have but fitting it into your life until it becomes more relevant. Passion in what you do is what brings us happiness, not some distant achievement in the future. And remember to have fun most of the time without losing focus on results; those who know me well know what I mean. That makes everything worth the effort and makes you wake up with a smile on your face.

A Wise man.

When I think about this story, it amuses me of how much an unpretentious thing can change the way a person lives his entire life.

It began with a Bubble Gum; I was 9 years old and really loved them. One time, my favorite brand added some phrases inside the gum's wrap, and one of them really got my attention: "A wise man asks himself; a fool asks the others."

Well, I wanted to become a wise person, so I should start asking things to myself; that is what I did. It did not take me too long to realize that I would end up asking things to other people at some point, but the real meaning behind those words was still valid: A wise person asks FIRST to himself and only then inquires others.

That phrase probably contributed for me to become an introvert, observe more, speak less, and be more considerate in my actions.

That really helped me my entire professional (and personal) life. Whenever I ask my colleagues questions, I usually already have some thoughts about it and even some suggestions. That is important if you want to be considered for leadership positions. On the other hand, it is also helpful when you have things to complain about and would like to change them. People generally do not like to receive complaints but will always respect you if you follow by suggestions on improving things.

Whenever your opinion is asked, do not just reply with yes or no, like it or do not like it; always explain the reasons for that and, whenever possible, also give suggestions. People around you will start doing the same for you, and there will be many gains for everybody. Show people around you that you can be a wise person.

Summing up, some of this advice really helped me throughout my professional life, and I would like to give them all at once to my younger self; maybe I could have achieved some things earlier in my life, and I would be really happy if at least one of them ended up helping you.

Actively work to develop your whole potential. Be a humble leader, care about your colleagues, and help them to evolve. Be a wise man, thoughtful of your actions, always asking yourself first what to do before asking others. Never be afraid of restarting your life because you may even find more success and happiness ahead.

Seek an everyday life full of achievements and have fun whenever possible.

About Paulo Corsi

Paulo aulo Corsi is Brazilian, born and raised in São Paulo. He started his professional life at 14 years old with his uncle as a clocksmith apprentice, where he learned a lot about the importance of processes and of every component in them. He became an Electronic Technician in High School and studied Business in Fundação Getúlio Vargas, widely known as one of the best Universities in the country, specializing in General Business Management and Marketing.

He almost always occupied leadership positions in different types of teams throughout his professional career, like sales, marketing, support, and debt collection.

He started his first own business at the age of 28 with basically only technical knowledge and goodwill, as it happens with many entrepreneurs that didn't work at all, and he had to start it all over again - but with a lot of new learnings on how not to do things. All his next business worked really well.

Now his focus is being the Executive Director for the east of the State of São Paulo for BNI, the largest international networking organization in the world, where he is also a leader of the International Advisory Council of Executive Directors.

In the networking area he created the concept of the Networking Quotient, a simple tool to assess your networking efforts and help you decide if you should expand your network or explore deeper the one you have. In 2018 he co-authored a book with the same title with his good friend YP Lai, published in English.

André Luís and Lara's proud father - two incredible persons – love traveling (especially nature), learning, helping people, cooking, being with friends, listening to music, and rarely refusing singing in a karaoke.

CHAPTER

Eight

With a little help from my friends

I am very happy where I am right now. I am comfortable with my choices and I worry that if I had to give advice to my younger self I would be reluctant to advise change. I would not advise how to change anything or how to do something different, yet I would advise myself on how to view the events that unfold and the decisions that I make as I grow into the person that I am today. A very different project is, using my life and business experience, to advise an entrepreneur who is starting his journey just how to progress.

One of life's gifts is our networks. The people we meet on our journey, particularly the people we keep with us in this period of our lives, is very important. The mentors we select create the footprints that we can either choose to follow or not, and it is this guidance that can accelerate success. We do not just learn from the people that get it right, though. Often, the more valuable lessons are from the people that got things horribly wrong. The advice that follows is a mixture of the path that I chose, and the advice given to me on my journey from the people who got things wrong and the ones who walked with me for a while and guided my success.

The first thing to bear in mind is that you can choose to follow someone's lead or to take their advice, and this is important. Wisdom comes by knowing who to listen to and who to follow, and although I can offer some advice on this, it is your biggest lesson and one that you must work out for yourself.

Quite often, we follow a route planned out for us by our upbringing, our circumstances, our education, or our first guides in life (our parents). The majority of us go into employment following education, and this is not a failing. It is important to learn these structured lessons but even more important to keep learning and keep an open mind and open eyes and ears during our lives. It is very smart to be coached and progress through a business education while being paid to do so. This provides us with many of our early trappings of success. If we are successful, then it is easy to stay in this environment longer, and the talent here is to know when the time is right to step away from the safety net. Not to go it alone but to strike out into self-employment and to take charge of your own destiny.

You will have experienced either a pull factor to make this step, where you are compelled to follow a dream/idea or a push factor. Quite often, you have seen a colleague take this step and do very well. This makes you wonder if you could do the same, and as this desire grows, you may save some money or minimize your outgoings in preparation? This is important as once the steady income disappears; you will need some money to survive until your venture takes flight. The longer you stay, the more you earn, and the less likely you will be to step away. Some people start on their own because of a push factor. This may be a redundancy or a boss that passes you over for promotion or a number of issues that you cannot face anymore.

I was pushed. I worked as a manager in a large format retail operation, and I owe a debt of gratitude to a very insecure boss that saw me and my rise as a threat to himself. My life was made challenging, and a bad day turned into a bad month and then a bad year. I decided to step away before I knew just quite what I was going to do. I had recovered from skin cancer just the year before and realized just how little time that we have in this life to be happy and make the right decisions. I may still have been employed and would not have had all of the amazing opportunities that my life has presented to me if I had stayed and been unhappy, just to take home a wage cheque each month. As I type this, I am compelled to share with you the steps that I took in taking charge of my life and its embracing opportunities.

Choose something that you have some knowledge of. You can research this and speak to people to find out how your chosen industry works and do not necessarily need to have intrinsic knowledge of the sector. This knowledge can build as you research and prepare. For me, it was floristry. My mom was a florist all of her life, and I even completed my University dissertation on this sector. If you wait for an original idea, then you will never start. This is very rare, and often, if no one has started this type of business, then there is a good reason, and this is a sign not to follow this path yourself. I chose a sector that was already catered for in my town; in fact, there were 3 very strong competitors just 4 miles from my shop. They all made fantastic floral arrangements and had been established for more than 10 years. To many, they saw that my decision was madness, yet to me, I saw 3 flawed business models that almost had it right. They were in a very expensive and exclusive high street location and, as such, needed to charge a price that absorbed their overheads. They were all focused on image and design, yet I saw that this was arrogant and not customer focused. Instead of selling the customer a great product that they chose at a great value price, they sold a great product that they wanted to sell at a premium price. I saw a gap in a market that they had stimulated, grown, led to maturity, and then focused on competing with each other rather than wowing their customers.

I formed a mission statement, and this was to **provide the best possible flowers at the best possible price for the customer while offering a service that exceeded their expectations.**

I found a vacant shop unit at the end of a row of shops on a busy precinct. The other tenants were traffic generators for my new venture, and it was a similar demographic to that where my competitors were. As it was a secondary location, the rent was cheaper, and the bonus was that there was plenty of free parking to attract customers away from the town centre. Oh, it was also on a busy road and could be seen clearly as cars passed by. The signage and shopfront became a free advert. This is another piece of advice. Keep your overheads low and your impact high.

It is important to know your strengths and play to them! I am not a financial expert or a legal wizard. I tried to save money in these areas, and this almost caused me big problems. It is an investment to spend money in these areas as it allows you to focus on your passion and to let the experts focus on theirs. I corrected this mistake a year later when I discovered BNI and never looked back from this point. I would revisit BNI later as it was the catalyst that transformed me and my business.

I needed skilled staff, and although I was lucky to have a mom that was a very skilled and well-known florist (Tina Sawdon), we soon needed more staff, and I discovered a skills gap in the industry. Many people wanted to be florists, they just were not trained, and I needed staff NOW.... We approached some retired florists and offered them flexible part-time hours. We also started training straight away, and from that point, we generated our well-trained staff that understood and lived our culture of absolute service. In an industry of technicians, we created a business of customer service experts. Retention and succession planning are key in this area, and I became paranoid about succession. If someone left or was ill, who would replace them? I had a plan for all outcomes, and my advice to you is to build this into your staff costs from day 1. If your technician leaves, do you still have a business? Never leave yourself exposed.

I approached a flower importer and discovered that he would offer me 30-day payment terms. This sounded very helpful, and then I started to think about the product that we were buying. Flowers are a fresh product, and you really need to sell your stock within 3-4 days to keep your stock fresh and attractive. When a customer walks into any business for the first time, they are making a purchase decision. If we impressed them with location, quality, price, and service, then why would they go anywhere else? I made a deal with the supplier. I would pay for my stock when I purchased it. This made me a very attractive customer to him as he carried no risk. I recognized that this had value, so I asked for a 5% discount on all stock as a thank you for my prompt payment. By the end of year one, this discount represented thousands of pounds of money that I kept on my bottom line. My advice here is to always think differently to your competitors. You do not have the burden of being conditioned to do something a particular way, as that is how it has always been done. Innovate and look for new ways to keep costs down as £1 saved is often worth £5 earned.

I had my business idea; I had carried out my research. I had my location, suppliers, and staff. Now I needed an image and an interior design. The business's name was flower house, and I spent a considerable amount with a graphic design agency to create our image. A number of agencies were asked to pitch for our work, and one of them stood out. The agency we chose was aligned with my white walls and ceiling image and a striking red logo. We stood out, and so did our colorful stock. We were good to go, now time to promote our business.

We did not have a huge budget for advertising, and so we created a whisper campaign and allowed the local residents to spread the word for us. I whitewashed the windows of the shop and just left the signup. I placed a large sheet of paper in the window with "30 days to go" on it and changed it every day as the countdown continued. I printed off some leaflets that simply said, "Flower house coming soon to 1 Harper Parade," and I spent my evenings distributing thousands around the local housing estates. Finally, I enlisted my friends to spend time in the local bars and coffee shops and ask strangers, "What do you think Flower house is going to be?" We made people talk, and we built anticipation on a shoestring budget. As we grew, we realized that our product was our advert and that for every product we sold, this was an opportunity to capture a new customer. As people received our flowers, we realized that we could incentivize them and compel them to use us in the future. This was our opportunity to grow, and someone was paying us to do this. My advice here is that you are your best advert, and no one is as passionate about your idea as you are. Back yourself and make sure that every pound you spend on advertising and promotion is well spent or measurable.

We trained the staff, and as we grew, the team trained the incoming team. We clearly allocated technician roles and customer roles, and every member of the team was trained to fully understand that the task at hand is never more important than the customer in the shop or on the phone. This did mean that staffing needed to be higher than originally planned, yet we viewed this as an investment. We never knowingly carried out a task at the expense of a paying customer that was waiting. All staff believed this, and it was part of our culture. We were not an established business, and as such (as previously mentioned), we needed to think carefully about how to attract staff. We offered flexible working and lots of school time or part-time hours; we even had a staff member who came in after the shop was closed and carried out some of the work as this fitted in with their personal circumstances. My advice here is to have a flexible approach with staffing, as this will help you retain staff that you have invested time in. Always recruit culture first and skill second as you can train skill, yet you cannot easily develop culture.

I have mentioned that customer service was the most important area of our business, and we never took focus away from this. When you are dealing with a fresh product, the thing can go wrong, and it is how you deal with these issues that do not just retain a customer, it creates a raving fan. Many florists would argue over how flowers were handled, where they were placed, or how long they had been out of the water should they have received a complaint. Flower house had a refund and replacement policy.

On one occasion, a customer was visiting his mom from out of town, and as he was leaving he came into the shop and personally selected "her favorite flowers" for us to deliver later in the day. Following delivery, the lady returned to the shop and complained about the selection and that there were not many flowers in the bouquet. This was true, correct. Her son did not want to spend very much, and this was reflected in his selection. Many florists would have argued this fact and done nothing to help but not flower house. We apologized and asked the lady to point out some of the flowers that she liked, and we made up a bouquet of these and presented them to her. The value was 5 times that of the son spent, and she went away happy without having to pay a penny more. We then called the son (our customer) and explained that his mom had been in the shop to complain. He panicked, and we quickly explained what we had done. He was relieved and not prepared for what happened next. We refunded his spending back onto his card and asked for his address. We sent a bouquet to him to apologize, and this completely exceeded all expectations. We captured a set of customers for life and some raving fans that became evangelical about our business. My advice here is to ALWAYS exceed customer expectations as this is an investment in your business's future and is a better value than any advertising that you could ever spend.

Throughout my journey, there has been a strong network of trusted advisors that have been on call at every step to offer support, suggestions, and guidance. I cannot separate my success from the success that I have had in this network. I chose to be part of BNI (Business Network International), and I thank Mike Carling from the MAP Group for pointing me in this direction. He opened up a world that changed me and my future for the business while allowing me the opportunity to help thousands of people in return. I have lived a life based on giving unconditionally, and this premise of "Givers Gain" is at the core of the BNI network. My final part of advice is to find a network that works for you, and I would obviously nudge you towards BNI as it changes and develops many businesses.

In summary, the advice that I give you is distilled into 16 points:

- Wisdom comes by knowing who to listen to and who to follow, and although I can offer some advice on this, it is your biggest lesson and one that you must work out for yourself.

- The trappings of employment can make it is easy to stay in this environment longer, and the talent here is to know when the time is right to step away from the safety net. Not to go it alone but to strike out into self-employment and to take charge of your own destiny.

- Save some money or minimize your outgoings in preparation? This is important as once that steady income disappears, you will need some money to survive on until your venture takes flight.

- Choose something that you have some knowledge of.

- If you wait for an original idea, then you will never start. These are very rare, and often, if no one has started this type of business, then there is a good reason, and this is a sign not to follow this path yourself.

- Form a mission statement (This is separate from a business plan).

- Keep your overheads low and your impact high.

- Know your strengths and play to them. Find people who complement you and fill those skill gaps.

- Never leave yourself exposed. Succession planning is important.

- Always think differently to your competitors. Innovate and look for new ways to keep costs down as £1 saved is often worth £5 earned.

- Invest in an expert to create your image.

- You are your best advert, and no one is as passionate about your idea as you are. Back yourself and make sure that every pound you spend on advertising and promotion is well spent or measurable.

- The task at hand is never more important than the customer in the shop or on the phone.

- Always recruit culture first and skill second as you can train skill, yet you cannot easily develop culture.

- ALWAYS exceed customer expectations as this is an investment in your business's future and is a better value than any advertising that you could ever spend.

- Find a network that works for you, and I would obviously nudge you towards BNI as it changes and develops many businesses.

About Russ Sawdon

Russ started a floristry business in the Teesside area, as his first venture into the world of business. Having sold it to the current owner, it continues to be successful and is still growing. Russ has a passion for helping and supporting people in all areas of life and business, and is a "Giver" by nature.

He was a proud member of BNI before, taking the role of Executive Director, Durham and Teesside Region, alongside his wife Gill. They have helped hundreds of companies share in many millions of pounds worth of revenue, with their BNI Region generating in excess of £12m of closed business last year.

During his time in BNI, Russ has trained hundreds of fellow Directors, served on the Franchise Advisory Council in the UK and also served as the first ever President of the Founders Circle, where he represented over 850 Executive Directors from around the world, as their contact with the Global Support Team.

The work that Russ does globally has been recognized by Dr Ivan Misner, Founder and Chief Visionary Officer of BNI, and Graham Weihmiller, Chairman and CEO, with awards for "Outstanding Contribution to the organization and Leadership". Russ always wants to make a difference and more importantly he wants to support you in doing the same.

Russ is the proud father of Harry,16 and Edward, 12, and the reluctant owner of a beautiful dog called Coco (The family insisted!). In the little spare time he has, Russ loves films, and you will often catch him watching his favourite film, Moneyball, yet again. Forty times so far, and counting!.

CHAPTER

Nine

YOU ARE THE CREATOR OF YOUR REALITY

"Whatever Your Mind Can Conceive and Believe, It Can Achieve."
– Napoleon Hill,

Book: "Think and Grow Rich," 1937

When I was young, my mother said to me: "Every person who crosses your path is there to teach you something." I'm continuously learning during my life, and I can say that I am my better version every day. I've learned how to observe myself through the reality that surrounds me, accept the contrast, and be eager for what's coming next.

I believe that we came into this life experience to live happily ever after. But in order to do so, we need to learn what makes us happy. To do so, we need to experience both good things and contrasts. We become masters of our reality when we start to be grateful for all. I see life as a gym: tougher it is, stronger you become. When we've learned the life lesson, we will close an old cycle to open a new one, a more fulfilling. I believe that if you want to recognize heaven, you have to have a walk-through hell first.

Knowing what makes us feel good and following our intuition will lead us to manifest that desire or even something better. We must ascent our awareness. If we really want to choose the path that will lead us to our best version of our future self, we need to listen to our intuition more.

Let me give you a little bit of my background. I was born in Yugoslavia. My mother was a teacher, and my father was a van driver for a producer of kids' shoes. I have a 12 year older brother and an 8 years older sister. Yugoslavia was a country, where till 1991 there was no entrepreneurship. All companies were run by the government and doing so, we were all equal, which was safe. I believe human beings are made to evolve and grow. And when my country Slovenia decided to be independent, there we started to evolve as entrepreneurs also. I was 10 at that time.

After different job experiences, I decided to work on my own, as I want, with the quality that I believed in, being free to innovate as I feel right after listening to potential customers. I was 28 when I started my career as an event organizer. And it was the beginning of the recession of 2009. My first thought was, if I can make it during these times, I can make it anytime. I started from scratch. I've chosen to be the only one to hold responsible for my success. I remember my mother asked me if I was not afraid of not having every month the safety of the salary. My answer was: "I may not have the certainty of receiving that small amount of money on my account every month, but I have every day the chance to earn much more. It totally depends on me." Taking responsibility gives you the power to change your path whenever you decide to do it.

The first struggle I had to deal with was to give the price for my work. I analyzed the efforts, the hours, the cost of my working hour, and the value that I was giving to customers, but I still felt bad when I had to provide them with the price. I realized that I felt bad due to limiting beliefs that came from my cultural background, like the belief that only men can be successful. Most of the limiting beliefs came from my family, where I was taught to work hard, earn a bit, and save it all for the bad times. Or: "We can't afford it." And others from the culture, such as, money is the root of all evil or money doesn't grow on trees. There was no concept of abundance and living the life that you want and deserve - just surviving. The feeling I had at that time was that I was not worthy and had to struggle. It was not about putting a price on my work; it was about giving value to myself.

The first book that helped me change this limiting belief was "The science of getting rich," written by Wallace D Wattles, published in 1910. Two books that helped me replace the old beliefs with the new ones were: "Secrets of the Millionaire Mind," by T. Harv Eker, published in 2005, and "Rich dad and poor dad" written by Robert Kiyosaki, published in 1997. Later on, I came across a book that helped me to understand how to manifest:

"Think and Grow Rich," written by Napoleon Hill in 1937 and the same period, I started to learn more about the law of attraction from Ester Hicks through numerous registrations published on Youtube.

Living with new beliefs brought me in 2 years to succeed and live the life I wanted. Just when I was wondering how to simplify the search for new customers, I came across BNI. Coincidence? No. I was ready for the new cycle of growth. And when the student is ready, the teacher appears: I was ready to meet BNI.

BNI could give me the tool to reach my potential customers easier. But joining BNI wasn't so easy. First, they didn't want to accept me to the core group where they started building a new Chapter because I was not local, and I didn't have any connection in this town. The second was that I couldn't spend the money on the membership fee. I was almost at the end of my year working circle, and I didn't put aside the marketing budget. What was interesting that I felt it deep inside that I had to be part of this community. I didn't understand exactly why and what could I expect. I just felt that behind that door was my new life. Somehow with my strong intention and showing the strong will, I convinced the Director Consultant to accept me. But there was another thing that I needed to do - find the money. A few weeks later,

I received a phone call. It was one of my customers that owed me some money for more than 2 years. I wasn't thinking anymore about it because thinking about it was making me angry. She apologized for the delay, and she said that she could not pay me the whole amount, but a good part of it. I thought better something than nothing, and I accepted it. The interesting part was that the amount she could pay was precisely the same amount as the membership fee. Coincidence? Nope. I raised my head towards the sky. I took this as a sign that I was on the right path. My feelings were full of gratitude and joy because a desire just came true.

In the third year of my solo career, everything was doing good. I was in my comfort zone. I was having a great experience of growth in BNI as a person and entrepreneur. I had the chance to meet new people and build a lot of strong relationships. I felt a sense of community and security because I was not alone anymore. My life was sailing smoothly. I gained self-esteem, and I was aware of my value. Since life is an evolutionary journey, I started to dream bigger. I was thinking of how I could improve my business to manifest my new desires. I was aware that with the same business, doing it in the same way, I wouldn't have accomplished my dreams. But I have to be honest. I didn't do anything about it.

And then, something unexpected happened. I had to cancel one of the main events due to the lack of sponsorships. Companies that used to invest money in the visibility on events started to lower their marketing budgets. The recession had hit me with the tail. At first, I felt lost. I was worried. I was searching for new opportunities. All this with a sense of fear. I knew that you cannot create something good out of a bad feeling. When I finished all the calls to announce that the event was canceled, I felt lighter. I relaxed a bit, and I took a deep breath. I was standing outside on the balcony. It was the beginning of March 2013. The spring was coming. So, I thought to enjoy the sun on my face, the spring breeze on my skin, and the view of this beautiful open sky. I turned my head up and just stared into the sky, and then, I got the flash! It all made sense! I said, "Thank you for this experience. I trust you that what is happening right now is for my greater good. Even if I cannot see it yet, I'll eventually get it why this experience was good for me. And I'm eager to receive what's coming next." In less than a week, someone asked me if I was interested in developing BNI in Italy, just across the border of my country. I felt that this was my new evolutionary circle. Not thinking about the fact that building communities for entrepreneurial success won't be easy at all! Since I felt safe and not alone in the BNI community, I knew that if I struggled,

I could always count on the people who live the Givers Gain philosophy.

It took me a year or so to sign the contract. When I was sitting there in front of the contract, I was thinking to myself: "You are still in time to change your mind. You know when you sign this, you have to do it. No matter how! What if you can't? You've tried it already, and nothing happened. What if you don't find people interested? Also, to mention that you are a young woman from a foreign country. From the country that Italians see as poor and underdeveloped. What can you teach them that they don't already know, and maybe even better than you?" I was trying to listen to my inner voice, the intuition, but the rational brain was so loud that I hardly understood what my emotional part of the brain was saying. Then I heard my mother's voice, that she used to say: "You are smart. You can arrange yourself in any situation, and you can achieve it all." I got the push: "Despite all fears, I want to do it! The only belief that I need is the belief in myself. And once again, my future depends on my commitment and my capabilities. And if I don't know how to do it, I can learn it. And no matter what, I will find the way!" So, I signed the contract.

I was in this state of mind because I passed almost a year to do the door-to-door activity, and I did approximately

200 meetings that ended with: "No, thanks." I couldn't find not even one person who wanted to commit to start a brand-new Chapter in a brand new Region. Every time I heard "No, thanks," I thought, what can I improve in my approach to receive a "Yes." I knew it that out there was the right person. I have to meet enough of wrong people, learn from them, to be ready when I meet the right one. I read somewhere the story of a little girl that was selling cookies. She had a strong motivation to earn money from that to go with her mother on vacation for the first time. Her lesson was: 3 times SW: "Someone will, someone won't (So What?), Someone is waiting." And it was just like this. When I met the first one that said yes, I improved my approach, I was much more self-confident, and my motivation became stronger. The voice in my head that tried to persuade me not to sign the contract was not only mine, some people tried to project their fears on me. They were trying to convince me not to go to Italy. Young, foreign woman, without connections, was the baggage that they tried to drop on me. "Only you know what you can be, do or have. No one else can know it for you," a thought came on my mind. I'm also stubborn, so the more they tried to persuade me, the more I was convinced that I have to do it. I used to say: "If you have a strong desire to do it, you will find the way." I couldn't give up at that point. My reputation for walking the talk was challenged.

A week later, that I signed the contract, I met an entrepreneur who had an IT company, who, after my 5 minutes long-lasting speech, said: "I wanna do it!" His eyes were shining. I was his solution, and he was mine! After another week, I received an e-mail from a real estate agent who wanted to know more about BNI. I met him in a pub and it was a pleasant surprise because he knew the reason for every single commitment. I called the IT entrepreneur, and despite his busy schedule, he was free and near the pub. It took just a few minutes to get him there. My first concern was if these two would get along with each other. And there we were, the three of us, complete strangers, drinking a beer together. We were talking about the strategy to build that first Chapter. A teardrop came down on my cheek—a tear of joy. I started to see it! This was the first step towards my vision coming true. My burning desire was about to take birth.

A week or two later, we were sitting together again. But this time was early in the morning, drinking coffee with 12 business owners who were listening to me with interest. Three new members joined on that day.

A week after the coffee meeting, it was the beginning of November; we started with informational meetings. From that time on, I had a morning ritual. Every morning I made a coffee, and I went out on the terrace to drink it.

I was facing brown trees without leaves, the green of the river passing by the house, and the sunrise of the new day with new opportunities that were about to be born. I was completely relaxed, and in this state of mind, I started to visualize how we were adding new members to this chapter. I knew exactly what I wanted. I asked for guidance through intuition, which would bring me new ideas and the right attitude to reach the goal. My mother told me once at a young age that people perceive you as you perceive yourself. At that time, I hadn't started from zero; I did it under zero! I came into a new neighboring country, Italy. I had no choice but to pursue a new path. I didn't have enough money to survive and build the new business at that time, so I borrowed it. I was actually completely broke. But no one noticed it. I thought that if I were showing them how to be successful, I needed to be successful first. And if I am broke, it doesn't mean that I'm not successful. I did many great things in my life. I was emitting success, even if it was a mental projection. I was living the emotions of my future self, right there in front of them.

It seemed that my rituals worked, because in only 7 weeks after the launch event, we put together 35 entrepreneurs, and doing so, we got the reward for the Hall of Fame launch Chapter, we were the first to do it in a brand new territory and the fastest. We also hit the record of the biggest launch event in Italy at that time. 330 new visitors registered at the event, which was more than double of the usual count of visitors at launch events.

This is a small proof that you have to live your future self-first with all of your senses, and only then it manifests. But the real proof I discovered just a year ago. Dott. Glen Rein wanted to prove that we can shape reality with our thoughts. He put DNA into test tubes with water. He made 3 groups of people that were holding in hand these test tubes. The first group had just had to focus on having a strong intent to change the DNA. Nothing happed. The second group made them feel strong emotions of love and gratitude. Nothing happened. But when they were inducted into the third group, feeling of love and gratitude, and then they added a strong intention, the DNA changed. Some DNA was wrapped or unfolded with a percentage of 25%, in only 2 minutes—source: The power of the quantum brain of J.L. Marshall & Italo Pentimalli.

To sum up. You have to know what you want and deserve, most importantly, how you want to feel in your future version. You have to live the emotions as it already happened. Then you have to listen to the gut instinct that is guiding you towards your goals. Your emotions are like a compass - do only what makes you feel good, and with people that make you feel good. Be aware of signs. Accept the contrast with the faith that there is something greater around the corner, but you have to learn the lesson first to be ready to receive it and manifest your desire.

You can be, do or have whatever you want. So, dream big and take action!

About Vera Dobravec

Vera Dobravec was born and raised in Slovenia, on the border with Italy. Curiosity leads her to learn new languages that allow her to meet people from different countries. She calls herself a citizen of the world. After she finished high school, she desired to travel, but she did not have money. So, she went to work on a cruise ship, where she learned the discipline and the importance of following her passions. At 22, with only € 50 in her pocket, she jumped on a truck to go to work in Madrid for two years, and later she spent another year in Tenerife, where she worked in a travel agency. Meanwhile, she graduated in Tourism

At 28, she started to organize corporate events in Slovenia. Another 5 years passed, until the desire to expand in Italy became a necessity. At that moment, confident that something greater awaited her outside the comfort zone, she accepted the opportunity to develop the franchise of the world's largest referral network - BNI. Starting from scratch again, and this time without any connections. If you want something, you will find a way to get it. She knocked on 200 doors until she found the first follower. At that point, she started a great business with constant growth. An organization that is changing the culture, replacing the competitive economy with a collaborative one. Her gratification is to see people fulfil their wishes. She lives life like it is a Christmas tree, under which some presents still need to be opened.

CHAPTER

Ten

Open your mind to all possibilities as you travel through time

My journey to entrepreneurship began back in 1982 when I was 6 years old. Yes, 6 years old! My parents had been running a tour business, Crown Tours, for many years, taking individuals to sporting events, like Nebraska Football, Major League Baseball, and others. Then, they decided to start a travel agency, Royal Travel. You might find yourself asking what that has to do with me. And the answer is absolutely everything. In the afternoons of my early days of grade school, I would walk to the travel agency and take lessons on the airline computer software. I passed the courses and could book an airline ticket before I was 7. This started me on the path that I am still on today.

Although my parents sold the Royal Travel, I continued to be part of their ongoing tour business throughout my high school years at Creighton Prep in Omaha, NE. As I entered college at Creighton University, my passion continued to be travel, but it evolved to be more than that. As I entered my second year at Creighton University, studying Finance and Accounting, I applied for and was accepted into the building manager program at the Skutt Student Center.

The building manager program was the first layer of managerial experience. I would be fortunate to receive it. In this program, students at Creighton had the opportunity to learn the foundations of management while also actually running the business side of the center. We began with a semester of education, learning the ins and outs of the service center. We had to work in every layer of the building, from information service to food service. This set us up to 'run' the building in the evenings and weekends when the day-to-day employees were off. It was a great experience, and I learned a lot. The director of the program and center became more than a boss; he was a friend, colleague, and mentor. I was lucky enough to be local to Omaha, so I was able to work a lot during the summer months and enjoyed all the aspects of management, human relations, and customer service.

As my college years were coming to an end, albeit early. I was fortunate to be able to take summer school and save some time and money by graduating with a Finance Degree from Creighton University in 3 years. I began looking forward and applying for jobs. I applied for positions in hotel management and other hospitality and travel-related industries. However, it was not meant to be. Then, the travel agency that I had literally cut my teeth in, came full circle, making its way back to me. The owner, who had purchased the agency from my parents, was aging and asked if I would be interested in buying the agency that my parents had started. In November 1998 I was the owner of a travel agency, a business owner at 22.

Let's be honest for a moment; it was not all it was cracked up to be. Two months before the sale was final, we received word that the airlines would begin capping commissions. So, instead of receiving a straight commission on the entire airline ticket, we would get the commission percentage up to a certain point, and it would stop there and be the same, regardless of how much that last-minute ticket or first-class ticket cost. This became a challenge for travel agents across the country, so you had to find ways to specialize and differentiate.

I found myself at a crossroads, the first of many more on the continuing road to be an entrepreneur. I loved to cruise, so I decided to specialize in cruises and began, like I did at age 6, to take cruise courses and attend cruise conventions. In addition to that, I looked at myself in the mirror and asked who my target market was and how I was different from the other 115 travel agencies in our market. What I came to realize is that my age was a big factor, and not in a bad way. Full disclosure, I was a young travel agency owner, 22 years old, and there were plenty of agents and agency owners with more experience in the travel business than I had days on the Earth. What they didn't know about me was how I learned the travel agency business at 6 years old.

I began to focus on the relationships that I had made through my high school and college years. The people I knew from those days were either single with vacation aspirations or dating on the road to an engagement and eventual planning of a honeymoon. So, I began to focus on them solely. When I did this, it took some time, but it paid dividends because I usually only knew one of the travelers. The other travelers became new markets every time I booked a trip, and they told their friends, family, and colleagues. I was onto something here, and I wanted to figure out how to share it farther and wider.

Every Friday for months, I would get a phone call from a family friend, Cindy. She would ask me how business was, if I were looking for more business and if I wanted to check out this group she met with. Seriously, every Friday for months. I always told her how business was; usually, it was mostly good. I told her, of course, I was looking for more business, but I told her that I was not interested in a meeting with a group. I had done this before, and it was not beneficial. But she didn't give up. She continued to check in with me every Friday. Finally, I decided I had to check out what she was up to as it was the only way

I could get her to stop calling me every Friday. I asked her for more details, but I promptly shut her down again. This group was meeting on Friday mornings at 7:00 AM. I didn't see 7:00 AM most days, let alone on a Friday. She scoffed at me, possibly for the first time in my life, adult life anyway. Then she uttered the words, "I will pick you up at your office at 6:45, and you won't stand me up."

She was correct. I wouldn't stand her up, but what happened from there would change my landscape forever, both in the travel business and as an entrepreneur. I met her on a Friday morning and attended this group with her. But I was closed off; you might say closed-minded. I went with one intention. I fully intended to tell her I went. I saw it; it wasn't for me. Thanks, but no thanks. To say I shocked myself was likely the understatement of the millennia, or at least of my existence. You never know who or what will cross your path if you are open to it and allow it.

When I walked in, I saw other businesspeople who were interested in me and in who I was. They asked me about my business and about my history in the business. Then, they asked me to talk about my business for the entire room to hear. "Tell the room who you are, what you do, and what differentiates you from your competitors." I stood up; I introduced myself; I told a brief piece of my story and how I defined my target market. This was odd to me. These people were all more interested in me than telling me what they did or how they could help me. I started to feel good about being there. Then, towards the end, one of the other people stood up and said Vince, I think I may have someone you should meet. They are getting ready to book a trip, they don't know what to do or where to go, and hearing you made me think that you are the right person for them. I was excited; I probably jumped out of my seat to say thank you. Then he said, but, and my heart sank for a brief moment. It seemed like it took an eternity to hear the next words he uttered. He went on to say, "You need to come back here again, and not 2 or 3 months from now, next week or 2 at the longest." I responded to him, saying I will certainly look at my calendar and do my best to make that happen.

Seriously, was I fooling anyone? I had nothing on my calendar at 7:00 AM ever, let alone a Friday morning. When the meeting came to a close, I was asked if I could stick around. I was at the mercy of Cindy since she picked me up. I sat down with a couple of the other people, and I was asked for my feedback. I remember thinking this was strange again. People cared what I thought and wanted my feedback. Then came the sell... okay, it was not anything bad, but I was asked, "Since you liked what you saw, and you're willing to come back, would you be willing to be part of "The First Omaha Chapter of BNI?" Wait; what? What was BNI, what was a chapter? What was I doing? So many things went through my head. I gave the standard, non-committal answer, "I think so, let me think about it." Monday morning came around, and when I went to my office, I looked over the information I was given and filled out an application for this group. I realized all of these people I met knew people just like my classmates. They knew people with expendable income, that wanted to travel, and some even knew people that were planning weddings.

The next week I turned in my application, and I was accepted to be part of the "First Omaha Chapter of BNI." It was fabulous meeting everyone and sharing the same passion they had for each other. It made me realize that my high school and college days were coming out of me through BNI now. In high school and college, the value of being a man for others was instilled in me. I knew what that meant during those days, but little did I know what it was going to mean to me moving forward in my adult life.

Over the course of the next 20 years, BNI became so much more to me, but it all started because I opened up. It would be easy to tell you the rest is history, but so much more happened. During the same time period,

I was invited to a Rotary meeting. I had been attending one right near my office that took place Monday's during lunch. I decided to look into more information about Rotary, but this particular group was not interested in having me as they had another travel agent. I guess there was no room for 2 of us. At the meeting, I had the pleasure of meeting someone who became a very good friend and business mentor to me. He said he was actually a member of another Rotary and I should visit. I said, great, and when and where does it meet. He said tomorrow morning at 7:00 AM. I remember thinking this was a bad dream. Two meetings at 7:00 AM in one week. So, of course, I went. I was open-minded now to an early morning meeting. Again, it was a great experience. Neither of these experiences would have been possible with the mindset I had for many weeks, or even months when Cindy would call me on Fridays. I opened my mind to see the world in different ways, from different perspectives, and yes, even at different times of the day.

A few years later, on September 11th, 2001, a day that every US citizens will remember and many others abroad, I awoke like I had for many Tuesdays and headed off to Rotary. During Rotary, we began to learn something had happened, or at that point was even just beginning to happen. Time froze, and many came to my travel agency's office as we watched in horror what was unfolding.

As the World Trade Center towers fell to the ground and the Pentagon smoldered, I remember thinking the travel business was in trouble. We, of course, learned this was an act of terrorism, but I realized the travel business might not be where I wanted to spend the rest of my professional life. Therefore, realizing my degree field was in finance, I thought maybe I should be doing something different.

Over the course of the next year, I researched, as I did for many years about travel, but this time it was about financial institutions, from a sales perspective. I researched companies, their products, their contracts with agents, and how the companies were looked upon in the community. At the same time, I began studying for my exams to become an insurance agent, and right in front of me, through BNI, there was the referral I had been looking for. The agent, and fellow BNI member, introduced me to an agency recruiter and said, "sometimes you need to let a racehorse run." Then in late 2002, November to be exact, I started a new career as a multi-line insurance agent, putting my finance degree to use. I continued to be part of the Rotary I joined. But BNI was different; there was already a Property Casualty Insurance Agent, a Life Insurance Agent, and a Financial Advisor in my chapter. If you are not aware, BNI only allows one person per professional classification, so I had the choice of representing Health Insurance or Supplement Insurance in my current chapter or starting a new chapter.

The open-minded attitude that I had led me to start a new chapter. Sure, it was comfortable to be with all the people that had helped me succeed in the travel business, but I was not really a specialist in either of those insurance markets, and I felt both of those classifications were extremely specialized. I did start a new chapter with some help from other individuals. And today, I continue to help other individuals doing the same.

Looking back at the first decision I made, to be more open-minded, attending a meeting with Cindy really had an immense impact on my life, both as an individual and as an entrepreneur.

About Vince Vigneri

Vince Vigneri, an only child of two only children, graduated from Creighton University (Omaha, NE), where they instilled his work ethic and core value of helping others succeed. His company, BNI Heartland, hosts a weekly podcast and a monthly blog. Vigneri's first business, a travel agency, introduced him to BNI in the late 90s. At 7 years old, he became a self-taught travel industry expert. After the events of September 11th, 2001, he made a career change to his degree field, finance, becoming a multi-line insurance agent. The constant remained BNI and when the initial opportunity to purchase the BNI franchise arose, he seized it.

Vince Vigneri, together with his wife, Kristina, operate 3 franchises for BNI in Nebraska, Wyoming, South Dakota, and Western Iowa. Vince has been an Executive Director since 2007 and has held roles on BNI's Global Training Team, BNI's Mastery Circle, and the US Support Team. The Vigneris have been members of BNI's Founder's Circle annually since 2009. Vince has spoken at 8 BNI US National Conferences, was a Keynote Speaker for BNI Brazil's first National Conference in 2014 and BNI Mexico's 8th National Conference in 2017! Vince helped educate hundreds of BNI Directors from more than 30 countries.

Vince and Kristina have been married since 2001 and reside in Omaha, NE with their two children, Roch and Addison. In his spare time, he enjoys playing a round of golf, bowling and running. Together, they attend many concerts and are avid sports fans, attending Nebraska Football, Creighton Basketball and Baseball games, and the College World Series.

About Book

Ten Entrepreneurs and their inspiring journeys to help you find yours!

The advice we should have given to our younger self became the base of this book.

Are you an entrepreneur or do you want to be one?

The journey to entrepreneurship is unfortunately lonely and unguided. We have lots of ups and downs, and many many years of hard work is called overnight success. This is not the rule of doing business we have unknowingly made it like that.

We have been lucky to have friends worldwide, who are entrepreneurs too. The ideas, inspiration, and stories you will read in this book are from South America, USA, Canada, Europe and Asia. You will read all the stories in this book and find common threads to get success worldwide.

We have been always discussing how different signs we got and followed to find our tracks to be successful.

This book is a compilation of inspiring journeys of entrepreneurs from different parts of the world.

In crucks, this book talks about more than 100+ years of experiences with running 15+ companies and helping more than 10000+ entrepreneurs every day, every week, every year and helping them to grow their businesses.

We live in a highly connected world and we all have the potential to work internationally. We just need to know how to build the right connections worldwide.

This book will help you take your dreams and business internationally.

Welcome to the GATEWAY to the WORLD!

NOTES

NOTES

NOTES